the Lessons

of the

Church Year

K. C. Hanson

PENTECOST 1

PROCLAMATION 6 | SERIES A

FORTRESS PRESS | MINNEAPOLIS

PROCLAMATION 6
Interpreting the Lessons of the Church Year
Series A, Pentecost 1

Scripture quotations, unless otherwise noted or translated from the Greek by the author, are from the New Revised Standard Version Bible, copyright © 1989 by the Division of Christian Education of the National Council of Churches in the U.S.A. and used by permission.

The lectionary readings in this volume are arranged specifically for use in 1996. The coordination of propers, Sundays in Ordinary Time, and Sundays after Pentecost may vary in other years where cycle A is used.

Cover design: Ellen Maly
Text design: David Lott

The Library of Congress has cataloged the first four volumes as follows:

Proclamation 6, Series A : interpreting the lessons of the church
  year.
        p. cm.
    Contents: [1] Advent/Christmas / J. Christian Beker — [2]
Epiphany / Susan K. Hedahl — [3] Lent / Peter J. Gomes —[4] Holy
Week / Robin Scroggs.
    ISBN 0-8006-4207-4 (v. 1 : alk. paper) — ISBN 0-8006-4208-2 (v.
2 : alk. paper) — ISBN 0-8006-4209-0 (v. 3 : alk. paper) — ISBN 0-8006-4210-4
(v. 4 : alk. paper).
    1. Bible—Homiletical use. 2. Bible—liturgical lessons,
English.
BS534.5P74 1995
251—dc20   95-4622
                                                                CIP

        Easter / Gordon Lathrop—ISBN 0-8006-4211-2 (v. 5: alk. paper)
        Pentecost 1 / K. C. Hanson—ISBN 0-8006-4212-0 (v. 6: alk. paper)
        Pentecost 2 / Clarice J. Martin—ISBN 0-8006-4213-9 (v. 7: alk. paper)
        Pentecost 3 / William Klassen—ISBN 0-8006-4214-7 (v. 8: alk. paper)

The paper used in this publication meets the minimum requirements of American National Standard for Information Sciences—Permanence of Paper for Printed Library Materials, ANSI Z329.48-1948.

Manufactured in the U.S.A.   AF 1-4212
00   99   98   97   96   1   2   3   4   5   6   7   8   9   10

Contents

Preface

On completing this project, my thanks must go first to Professor Bruce J. Malina and Diane Jacobs-Malina. They not only acted as supportive colleagues this past year, but also as friends of the most valued kind. I am also grateful for the support and input of my friends and colleagues in The Context Group: Project on the Bible in Its Cultural Environment. This is an international group of biblical scholars (from the U.S.A., Canada, Scotland, Norway, Germany, and South Africa) who integrate social-scientific models in the exegetical enterprise, and who find creative ways to encourage and support one another in our work and lives. And finally, I want to acknowledge my mother, Gertrude Hanson, and late father, Kenneth C. Hanson, for their love and support, and from whom I first learned to read and study the Bible and to love the God of whom it speaks.

SUGGESTED READING

Since most of the Gospel lectionary readings are from Matthew, I have occasion in this volume to refer repeatedly to research I have done on that Gospel. These articles will appear in late 1995 in issues of *Semeia*: one volume on honor and shame in the Bible (Victor H. Matthews and Don C. Benjamin, editors), and the other on ritual studies and the Bible (Mark McVann, editor):

> "How Honorable! How Shameful! A Cultural Analysis of Matthew's Makarisms and Reproaches." *Semeia* (1995).
> "Transformed on the Mountain: Ritual Analysis and the Gospel of Matthew." *Semeia* (1995).

To read the Bible in the modern world, one must learn to enter its foreign world. The distance between the Bible and us is not only linguistic, geographical, and chronological, but, most dramatically, cultural. The following eight volumes constantly inform my own work (including the present volume) with regard to these foreign cultures, and I would recommend them for every pastor's and homilist's library:

> Duling, Dennis C. and Norman Perrin, *The New Testament: Proclamation and Parenesis, Myth and History*, 3rd ed. (Fort Worth: Harcourt Brace Jovanovich, 1994).
> John H. Elliott, *What Is Social-Scientific Criticism?* Guides to Biblical Scholarship (Minneapolis: Fortress Press, 1993).

William R. Herzog II, *Parables as Subversive Speech: Jesus as Pedagogue of the Oppressed* (Louisville: Westminster/John Knox Press, 1994).

Bruce J. Malina, *The New Testament World: Insights From Cultural Anthropology,* rev. ed. (Louisville: Westminster/John Knox Press, 1993).

Bruce J. Malina and Richard L. Rohrbaugh, *Social-Science Commentary on the Synoptic Gospels* (Minneapolis: Fortress Press, 1992).

Victor H. Matthews and Don C. Benjamin, *Social World of Ancient Israel 1250–587* BCE (Peabody, Mass.: Hendrickson, 1993).

Jerome H. Neyrey, editor, *The Social World of Luke-Acts: Models for Interpretation* (Peabody, Mass.: Hendrickson, 1991).

John J. Pilch and Bruce J. Malina, editors, *Biblical Social Values and Their Meaning: A Handbook* (Peabody, Mass.: Hendrickson, 1993).

I have occasionally referred to parallels in the *Gospel of Thomas*. This work is available in several translations, including:

Bentley Layton, *The Gnostic Scriptures* (Garden City, N.Y.: Doubleday, 1987).

Robert J. Miller, editor, *The Complete Gospels: Annotated Scholars Version*, 2nd ed. (Sonoma, Calif.: Polebridge Press, 1992).

James M. Robinson, general editor, *The Nag Hammadi Library* (3rd rev. ed.; San Francisco: HarperCollins, 1990).

The abbreviation for the *Gospel of Thomas* is *Gos. Thom.*, followed by a numbered saying (it includes 114 sayings in all). The *Gospel of Thomas* is a "sayings Gospel" rather than a narrative Gospel like those in the canon. The earliest Greek fragments of *Thomas* are from the third century, and the complete text in Coptic is from the fourth century, but many scholars now believe that much of it derives from 70–100 C.E. during the same period the canonical Gospels were written.

TERMINOLOGY

When discussing the people of the ancient states of Israel (the northern kingdom) and Judah (the southern kingdom) in the periods prior to Roman Imperial control, the terms *Jew* and *Jewish* are anachronistic; when referring to the people of the south, I employ the term *Judahites*. For the Roman era (after 63 B.C.E.) I use the word *Judeans* as the translation of the Greek term *Ioudaios*. But the reader should also understand the multivalent usage of that term in the ancient world: (1) those who live within the Roman province of Judea (as opposed to Galilee, Perea, Decapolis, etc.); (2) all those who identify themselves in relationship to the region of Judea, the traditions of ancient Judah, and/or the state religion of Judea and the Jerusalem temple and priesthood, wherever they lived throughout the Mediterranean and Middle Eastern world—even those who had joined a Jesus group; and (3) the Judean authorities. The term *Jew* rightly refers to the later eras when Judaism was defined in terms of the Babylonian Talmud and rabbinic authority (after 500 C.E.).

But if the residents of Judea are not most appropriately called "Jews," then neither are the earliest followers of Jesus or the many groups that grew up in the first and early second centuries rightly called "Christians." The term *Christianoi* is used in the New Testament only three times, and only as a word employed by "outsiders" (Acts 11:26; 26:28; 1 Pet. 4:16), along with "the Nazarene sect" (*Nazôraiôn haireseôs*, Acts 24:5). When discussing the period of Jesus' ministry, one might refer to his followers as the "Jesus faction," "Jesus followers," or "Jesus messianists." The main label one finds as a self-reference in the book of Acts is "the Way" (see, e.g., Acts 19:23; 24:14, 22), but "Jesus groups," "church" (e.g., Acts 5:11; 1 Cor. 6:4), or "churches" (e.g., Rom. 16:4; 1 Cor. 7:17) would also be appropriate. The reason for avoiding "Judaism" and "Christianity" and related terms for this era is that they mislead the reader into notions of centralized and normative "religions" that are appropriate only for later centuries.

COMMENTS

If readers want to make comments or ask questions about my analysis of texts, I can be reached on E-mail at: "kchanson@creighton.edu"; or by mail at: Dr. K. C. Hanson, Department of Theology, Creighton University, Omaha, NE 68178.

Pentecost Sunday
The Day of Pentecost
Whitsunday

Lectionary	First Lesson	Psalm	Second Lesson	Gospel
Revised Common	Acts 2:1-21 *or* Num. 11:24-30	Ps. 104:25-34, 35b	I Cor. 12:3b-13 *or* Acts 2:1-21	John 20:19-23 *or* 7:37-39
Episcopal (BCP)	Acts 2:1-11	Ps. 104:25-37 *or* 33:12-15, 18-22	I Cor. 12:4-13	John 20:19-23 *or* 14:8-17
Roman Catholic	Acts 2:1-11	Ps. 104:1, 24, 29-31, 34	I Cor. 12:3b-7, 12-13	John 20:19-23
Lutheran (LBW)	Joel 2:28-29	Ps. 104:25-34	Acts 2:1-21	John 20:19-23

FIRST LESSON: ACTS 2:1-21; NUMBERS 11:24-30; JOEL 2:28-29

Acts 2:1-21, the central narrative of the Pentecost tradition tells of the dramatic outpouring of God's Spirit on the followers of Jesus in Jerusalem fifty days following Jesus' passion and resurrection during Passover. And this takes place not just on the Twelve (including Matthias), but also on the one hundred and twenty plus (1:15). This is important for interpreting the pervasiveness of God's Spirit on these followers: it is not restricted solely to the Twelve of Jesus' inner circle.

The Gospel narratives climax at the Israelite season commemorating Yahweh's *deliverance* from Egypt, connected with the pastoral custom of lamb-slaughter and the agrarian festival at the beginning of the barley harvest. Acts, on the other hand, connects the outpouring of God's Spirit with the Feast of Weeks/Pentecost, signifying the climax of the barley harvest (Lev. 23:15-21; Deut. 16:9-11), and care of the widow, orphan, and sojourner as a commemoration of Israel's social marginalization as Egyptian slaves (Deut. 16:12). These are complementary as deliverance and community formation (see v. 21).

The narrator draws upon other Israelite/Judahite traditions in this narrative that help the reader understand the importance of the narrative action. First, the members of the Israelite crowd (who are gathered in Jerusalem from all over the Mediterranean and Middle East) hear these followers of Jesus speaking in their various native tongues (vv. 4, 6, 8, 11). This amazing phenomenon functions as a reversal of the confusion of tongues and scattering of peoples at Babel (Gen. 11:1-9).

Second, the manifestation of God's presence as a rushing wind and fire (vv. 2-3) recalls Yahweh's descent upon Sinai (Exod. 19:18), but especially Philo's account of the Decalog's revelation: "it was a rational soul, clear and distinctive, which fashioned the air and stretched it out and changed it into a kind of flaming fire, and so sounded forth a loud and articulate voice, like a breath passing through a horn" ("On the Decalog" 33). Related to this is Ezekiel's vision: "As I looked, a stormy wind came out of the north: a great cloud with brightness around it and fire flashing forth continually" (Ezek. 1:4); and, from the Pseudepigrapha (noncanonical Judean writings) is Enoch's vision of God, whose throne was surrounded by flames and whose face was obscured by fire (*1 Enoch* 14:21-22). Third, the quotation of Joel's prophecy regarding the pervasive bestowal of God's Spirit (Joel 2:28-32, quoted in Acts 2:17-21) casts the manifestations of the Spirit and creation of the community of believers as the fulfillment of prophecy, and therefore the actions of God rather than the actions of humans (see also Luke 3:16; Acts 1:5).

Repetitions highlight the descriptions of both the Spirit and the crowd. The house was filled (*pleroô*) with a mighty wind (v. 2); the Jesus group was filled (*pimplêmi*) with the Holy Spirit (v. 4); and they were accused of being filled (*mestoô*) with wine, rather than the divine (v. 13). These highlight (through three different words) that the place and the community were indeed filled up with *something* other than themselves. The reactions of the crowd are also repeated: they were "bewildered" (v. 6), "confused and wondered" (v. 7), "confused and perplexed" (v. 12), and some "were mocking" (v. 13). The repetitions of filling and bewilderment together indicate to the reader that the phenomenon was ambiguous and not self-explanatory. Peter's quotation and interpretation of scripture was required to clarify its meaning.

Unlike the ecstatic experience of the seventy elders in Numbers 11 (see below), the narrator identifies these wondrous utterances as articulate speech. Indeed, what they are declaring are "God's mighty deeds" (v. 11). But the text as a whole seems to point in two directions simultaneously: the disciples were proclaiming, while some of the crowd mistook this as simple drunkenness (v. 13)! Prophecy as *divine proclamation* is thus juxtaposed to (or interwoven with) prophecy as *ecstatic speech.*

Combining themes of divine presence, ecstatic prophecy, empowerment, and jealousy, **Numbers 11:24-30** depicts the bestowal of God's spirit on community leaders. What was previously given only to Moses is here more widely distributed to other representatives of the community, the seventy elders. The "prophesying" they did was evidently not in the mode of Amos or Isaiah—proclaiming God's message of judgment or deliverance to the community—but more likely an altered state of consciousness. This is the type of ecstatic experience Samuel predicted Saul would undergo among the band of prophets at Gibeah: "Then the spirit of Yahweh will rush upon you; and you will prophesy with them, and you will be turned into another man" (1 Sam. 10:6; see also 19:23-24; Jer. 29:26; 1 Cor. 12:10; 14:1-33).

The cloud is the form in which Yahweh's presence is revealed here. Along with fire, this mode of theophany (divine manifestation) runs throughout the Exodus and Sinai materials. The cloud-pillar proceeded before the Israelites by day on their way out of Egypt (Exod. 13:21-22); Yahweh appeared in a cloud to give the Israelites instructions (Exod. 16:9-12); Yahweh met Moses in a cloud on the mountain (Exod. 24:15-18); Yahweh's presence in the tabernacle appeared as a cloud on the mercy seat (Lev. 16:2); and Yahweh used the cloud over the tabernacle as a signal for the Israelite encampment or procession in the wilderness (Num. 9:15-23). In the priestly materials an interesting link is also made between Yahweh's presence in the cloud and the cloud of incense (Lev. 16:13). The cloud image as theophany appears in other contexts as well: Isa. 19:1; Jer. 4:13; Ezek. 10:3-4; Pss. 18:11; 104:3.

And like Yahweh in the Old Testament (Ps. 68:4), in ancient Ugaritic literature Baal is also called the "Rider on the clouds." This image of Yahweh and Baal as riding clouds like a chariot is connected to their exalted status, their control of the elements (like rain), and their mode of interaction with their human communities. The power of the cloud image as a focalizing symbol for divine presence lies in its characteristics as vaporous and elusive, coming from the sky, and alternatingly opaque and transparent. Clouds continue in modern times to move writers to reflect on their elusiveness:

> I've looked at clouds from both sides now,
> from near and far, and still somehow
> it's clouds' illusions I recall;
> I really don't know clouds at all.
> (Joni Mitchell, "Both Sides Now")

As the cloud is uncontrollable and unpredictable, so is God's presence. The story functions as an account of the initiation of the seventy elders appointed to aid Moses in administration. Like Saul's experience of the divine spirit before he takes office as king, the elders have an intense, transcendent, shamanlike experience at their initiation. They are overwhelmed and empowered by Yahweh's spectacular presence. Secondarily, it may also serve to legitimate Israelite ecstatic prophets as rooted in the Mosaic era (that is, this is part of Israel's "ancient" heritage, not a new phenomenon in the period of the monarchy).

Ritually, the narrative follows the elders through the three stages of a status transformation ritual (such as baptism, marriage, ordination), as articulated by Arnold van Gennep and Victor Turner. First, the elders are *separated* from the community as a whole and positioned in the sacred space of the tent (v. 24). Second, while in this state and space of liminality (threshold and margin), they are given the spirit of Yahweh and *transformed* in a unique experience (v. 25). During this liminal stage, Turner tells us to expect that the group in the liminal state experiences (among other things): a sense of the holy, an absence of hierarchy, a sense of *communitas*, and anonymity. And finally, they are *reaggregated* with the community in their new status and functions (v. 30). (For more on ritual transformation, see below on the First Sunday after Pentecost [Matt. 28:16-20], and the Second Sunday after Pentecost [Matt. 7:21-29]).

The prophetic words of deliverance in **Joel 2:28-29** stand as the climax to a long section proclaiming the renewal of the land and crops as well as the end of foreign oppression and of Judah's shame (vv. 18-27). The outpouring of Yahweh's spirit is promised for "all flesh," but the prophet is clearly using this phrase in a more restrictive sense than the rest of the Bible. In most cases this phrase encompasses not only all humans, but all animals as well (see, e.g., Gen. 6:19; Num. 16:22; Ps. 136:25; Jer. 32:27; Sir. 40:8; John 17:2). Joel, however, seems to employ the phrase to encompass only all the *Judahites.*

The most significant categories of social stratification are also articulated: male and female, old and young, slave and free. But what is important about the prophet's introduction of these categories is that Yahweh's spirit encompasses all of them; Yahweh now chooses not to discriminate in line with cultural expectations (see Gal. 3:27-28). In contrast to the need of dividing the spirit bestowed upon Moses (Num. 11:25), here the metaphor implies the spirit is in a liquid state that permeates the whole community like oil. This hearkens back to Moses' wish that all the Israelites would prophesy and receive the divine spirit (Num. 11:29).

PSALM 33:12-15, 18-22; 104:1, 24-35

Psalm 33 is a hymn, celebrating Yahweh as both creator of the universe and patron-god of Israel. The opening line used here (v. 12) begins with a "beatitude" or "makarism" (from Greek *makarios*), not a blessing (see, e.g., Pss. 1:1; 112:1; Matt. 5:2-12). Its force is not blessing, happiness, or good fortune, but honor: read "How honorable is the country whose deity is Yahweh!" This is a political-religious expression of Israel's patron/client relationship with Yahweh.

This declaration of praise and honor is juxtaposed to affirmations of Yahweh's role as creator, who watches from the skies and fashions human hearts. But all the terms for "seeing" also point to the ancient Mediterranean belief in the benevolent eye of God that counteracts the destructive powers of the "evil eye," usually manifested as envy (see, e.g., Deut. 15:9; Sir. 14:8-10; Gal. 3:1; note that English translations often obscure the phenomenon of the evil eye). Yahweh "looks down" (v. 13a), "sees" (v. 13b), "watches" (v. 14a), "observes" (v. 15b), and finally "Yahweh's eye is on those who fear him" (v. 18). This rich vocabulary of "seeing" speaks to God's care, provision, and protection of the community. God truly *sees* in all its senses: observation, perception, and depth of understanding.

Psalm 104 is a hymn, a song of praise. Unlike genres that are composed for specific rites, hymns are adaptable to a wide variety of worship settings. Their focus is the person and work of Yahweh—who Yahweh is, and what Yahweh has done. This is a creation hymn, praising Yahweh for all aspects of the created order: mountains and valleys; clouds and winds; waters and skies; animals of the land, sky, and sea; plants and trees; wine, oil, and bread; sun and moon. The second part of the hymn may be structured in the following manner:

A. Praise Summation	24-26
B. Description: Yahweh's power	27-30
1. Yahweh as food source	27
2. Provision	28
3. Non-provision	29
4. Creative Spirit	30
C. Series of Wishes	31-35b
1. For God	31-32
2. For the psalmist	33-34
3. For the wicked	35a+b
D. Concluding Call to Praise	35c+d
1. Personal	35c
2. Communal	35d

The hymn as a whole relates to this season in terms of God's creativity and spark of life. Most particularly, v. 30 articulates the creative force of God's Spirit or breath. All things have life only as God grants it.

SECOND LESSON: I CORINTHIANS 12:3-13

In the second major section of this Pauline letter to the Corinthians (1 Corinthians 7–15), Paul addresses specific questions about which this congregation has written him. He begins many of his responses with the phrase "Now concerning . . ." (Gk. *Peri de*; see also 16:1, 12):

"Now concerning the matters about which you wrote . . ." (7:1)
"Now concerning virgins . . ." (7:25)

"Now concerning food sacrificed to idols . . ." (8:1)
"Now concerning spiritual gifts . . . ." (12:1)

Chapters 12–14, then, address questions of "spiritual gifts" or "spiritual persons" (the Greek term *pneumatikôn* could mean either), which covers those who speak in tongues, interpret tongues, prophesy, heal, speak words of wisdom, speak words of knowledge, work wonders, and discern spirits (12:8-11). In 12:28 most of this list is placed after the roles of apostle, prophet, and teacher (all leadership roles).

The contrast of the sayings "Jesus is cursed!" and "Jesus is Lord!" is startling. Were there Corinthians who in ecstatic frenzy cried out the first blasphemy? Or is Paul just providing an ironic, shocking contrast to the affirmation of faith? The modern reader is given insufficient context to say what is going on here. (For other examples of "Jesus is Lord" as an early creed, see Rom. 10:9; Phil. 2:11.) This is a reminder that one is reading a letter between Paul and a congregation whom he knew well. Paul's letters contain many things that would require no explanation to audiences such as the Corinthians: they had originally been taught by Paul (Acts 18:1-17; 1 Cor. 2:1-5; 3:6; 4:14-16); Paul had made return visits (2 Cor. 12:14); the Corinthians had written and received letters from him (1 Cor. 5:9; 7:1; 2 Cor. 2:3-4); and oral messages had been sent and received through emissaries (see 1 Cor. 1:11; 4:17; 9:3; 16:10; 2 Cor. 8:6).

The main point in this section is that the diversity of God's gracious gifts (Gk. *charismata*) are manifestations of one Spirit. The unity of God's action and the consequent unity of the church are highlighted by the repetitions in this passage of the words *same* (same Spirit, same Lord, same God) and *one* (one Spirit, one body) (see also Rom. 12:3-8; Eph. 4:1-7). The necessity for Paul to make this argument is due to the rampant and destructive factionalism of the Corinthians. The divisions to which Paul refers are both factions identified by different leaders (see 1 Cor. 1:10-13; 3:5-9), as well as divisions based upon heritage and social standing: "Judeans and Greeks, slaves and free" (12:13; see also 7:17-24). This is a call to work together on the basis of their common infusion of God's spirit. Their diversity should not be used as a rationale for division, but as an exciting possibility of complementarity.

The Corinthians seemed to have been continually plagued with problems of internal strife based on their diverse understandings of "spirituality." They were "not lacking in any spiritual gift" (1 Cor. 1:7), and Paul had "sown spiritual things" among them (9:11). But Paul concluded that he still had to address them as "flesh-folk" rather than "spiritual-folk" who had to be fed on milk rather than solid food (3:1-3).

GOSPEL: JOHN 20:19-23; 7:37-39; 14:8-17

John 20:19-23. Of all the Gospels, John includes the most postresurrection narratives:

1. the discovery of the empty tomb (20:1-10);
2. Jesus' appearance to Mary Magdalene (20:11-18);
3. Jesus' appearance to the disciples (20:19-23);
4. Thomas's dispute and Jesus' appearance (20:24-29);
5. Jesus' appearance to the seven disciples at the Sea of Tiberias/Galilee (21:1-14);
6. the "call" of Simon Peter (21:15-19);
7. a dialog about the beloved disciple (21:20-23).

These are called "postresurrection" narratives because none of the canonical Gospels includes a narrative about the resurrection itself; this does not appear in Jesus-messianic literature until the *Gospel of Peter* (10:39-40), probably from the mid-second century.

Although different in several key respects, the closest parallel to this story in the Synoptic Gospels is Luke 24:36-49; but the parallels are, for the most part, not at the verbal level, but at the level of motifs. The parallel motifs are:

a. the setting on the first day of the week (Luke 24:1, 13, 33, 36; John 21:19);
b. Jesus' startling appearance in a room (Luke 24:36-37; John 21:19);
c. his greeting of "peace" (Luke 24:36; John 21:19, 21);
d. the disciples' fear (Luke 24:37; John 21:19);
e. the display of his hands and feet (Luke 24:39-40; John 21:20);
f. the promise or bestowal of the Spirit (Luke 24:49; John 21:22);
g. the forgiveness of sins (Luke 24:47; John 21:23).

But the bestowal of the Spirit for Luke is postponed until Pentecost, so only an oblique promise is made in 24:49. In John, on the other hand, the resurrection and the gift of the Spirit are integrated (but notice that Thomas is not on the scene to receive the Spirit with the other ten).

It is worth noting an important aspect of the Johannine conclusion: in all these post-resurrection narratives, *the evangelist never closes a scene with Jesus leaving.* In 20:17-18 Jesus directs Mary to announce to his disciples his ascension (not resurrection), and she leaves. John 20:19-23; 20:24-29; 21:15-19; and 21:20-23 all end on Jesus' words. And 21:1-14 ends with Jesus giving the disciples bread and fish. Although Jesus refers to the ascension (20:17), the evangelist never provides a narrative, as in Luke 24:50-53 and Acts 1:6-11. The point is that the evangelist uses this narrative technique to emphasize Jesus' enduring presence with his community: *he repeatedly arrives, but never leaves!*

John 7:37-39. John situates this Jesus saying on the last day of "the festival," referring to the Feast of Booths or Tabernacles (Heb. *Sukkoth*), the seven-day harvest festival in the fall (see Lev. 23:33-36, 39-43; Num. 29:12-38; Deut. 16:13-15; Neh. 8:13-18), later called Pentecost. The saying itself is rather obscure: Jesus invites believers to "drink." Even the reference to Scripture here is somewhat confusing. Rather than a simple scriptural quotation, the "quote" and the narrator's interpretation seem to be a midrashic combination of Isa. 44:3 and Zech. 14:8:

> For I will pour water on the thirsty land,
>   and streams on the dry ground;
> I will pour my spirit upon your descendants,
>   and my blessing on your offspring. (Isa. 44:3)

> On that day living waters
>   shall flow out from Jerusalem. (Zech. 14:8a)

The narrator then interprets the meaning of the saying, not as a call to follow Jesus, but as a prediction of the Spirit pouring out on believers. So this saying is placed here in a saying set in Jerusalem as a foreshadowing of the narrative in John 20:19-21 (see below). That he also sets the saying on Tabernacles/Pentecost ties John's reference to the bestowal of the Spirit to the narrative in Acts 2.

The Jesus speech in **John 14:8-17** is prompted in the narrative by Philip's request to "see the Father" (v. 8). Jesus' response begins with a series of rhetorical questions expressing incredulity: "Have I not been with you so long . . . ?" (v. 9a); "How can you say . . . ?" (v. 9b); and "Do you not believe . . . ?" (v. 10a). Jesus cannot comprehend that his unity with the Father has not been communicated clearly to the disciples.

The vocabulary that runs throughout John's Gospel is conspicuous here: *know, see, believe, works, receive, love, glory, the Father,* and *the Counselor.* Other than "the Counselor" as a term for God's Spirit, these words are not unique to John. But the other Gospels do not use them with nearly the frequency or with the distinctive nuances that John gives them. The Johannine themes that are touched upon in this brief passage are: (1) the oneness of Jesus and the Father (vv. 10-11; see 10:30; 17:11, 21-23); (2) Jesus' authority derives from the Father (v. 10b; see 4:34; 5:30; 6:38-40); (3) prayers in Jesus' name will be answered (vv. 13-14; see 15:7, 16; 16:23-24); and (4) the Father will send the Counselor (vv. 16-17; see 14:26; 15:26-27; 16:7-11).

HOMILETICAL CONSIDERATIONS

A sequence of increased openness and broader circles of inclusion can be seen in the biblical narratives. In the earliest Torah narratives, Moses alone receives Yahweh's spirit. In Numbers 11 this is extended to the seventy elders as representatives of the Israelites, but with the wish for it to be more widespread. In the postexilic prophecy of Joel, Yahweh's spirit is promised to all the other Judahites as well. In John 20, Jesus breathes the Holy Spirit on ten of the disciples. And in Acts 2, Peter proclaims the fulfillment of this prophecy for the early community of Jesus followers. But even this passage points toward further developments of this trajectory of inclusiveness when God's spirit is bestowed on Samaritans (Acts 8:14-17) and then Gentiles (Acts 10:1-48).

It is fundamental to understand that God's spirit is not something other than God. It is the language both Israelite/Judahite and Christian Scriptures use to speak of God's presence in a person or the community of faith (Acts 6:5; 11:24). So God's spirit rushes upon Israel's heroes for battle leadership (Judg. 6:34), signals royal empowerment (1 Sam. 16:13-14), throws prophets into ecstatic states (1 Sam. 10:9-13), geographically transports prophets in visions or otherwise (Ezek. 3:12-15; 11:22-24), whisks prophets into the heavens (2 Kgs. 2:16), emboldens disciples to proclaim the gospel (Acts 4:8-12, 31), empowers believers to speak in tongues (Acts 10:44-48), and prompts prophetic utterance (Acts 11:28). God's spirit, then, signals the divine will in all its various aspects. Humans cannot control it, predict its movements, or co-opt it. God empowers whom God chooses, where God chooses, when God chooses. And the texts above display an increasing awareness of how large the circles are of God's inclusive empowerment and relationality.

But the most extraordinary manifestations of God's spirit are in relationships: the creation of community, joy, generosity, and praise (Acts 2:46-47). The value systems of Western societies emphasize, not only the priority, but the supremacy of individualism and capitalism. Despite the positive aspects of these values, they often conflict with building a sense of relationality and community, and encouragement of generosity and hospitality. If our sense of self and self-worth derive from our economic security and individual achievement, we live on a flimsy foundation and set up barriers to God's creative acts. And the most amazing thing about the texts above is that they demonstrate how unexpectedly God's presence breaks into human experience.

First Sunday after Pentecost
The Holy Trinity
Trinity Sunday

Lectionary	First Lesson	Psalm	Second Lesson	Gospel
Revised Common	Gen. 1:1—2:4a	Psalm 8	2 Cor. 13:11-13	Matt. 28:16-20
Episcopal (BCP)	Gen. 1:1—2:3	Psalm 150 or Canticle 2 or 13	2 Cor. 13:(5-10) 11-14	Matt. 28:16-20
Roman Catholic	Exod. 34:4b-6, 8-9		2 Cor. 13:11-13	John 3:16-18
Lutheran (LBW)	Gen. 1:1—2:3 or Deut. 4:32-34, 39-40	Psalm 29	2 Cor. 13:11-14	Matt. 28:16-20

FIRST LESSON: GENESIS 1:1—2:4A; EXODUS 34:4-6, 8-9; DEUTERONOMY 4:32-34, 39-40

Genesis 1:1—2:4a. The symmetry and formulaic construction of this grand passage do not detract from its elegance, but enhance it. The creation narrative that follows in 2:4b—3:24 manifests the drama and humor of storytelling, employing setting, characters, dialog, and plot. But the "drama" of Genesis 1 derives from the majesty of liturgy.

The introduction (1:1-2) acts as both preamble and summary. As preamble it indicates the beginning situation: *tohu wabohu*, "formless and void," with God's spirit (or divine wind) hovering over the waters of this chaos. The question becomes: What can God do to bring shape, substance, and order where none of these exist? For the presupposition of this text is God's presence; without God's word and deed, and without God's creativity (in its fullest sense), it will remain chaos. And as summary, it encompasses the creation of "the heavens and the earth," the Hebrew expression for the whole universe.

The conclusion (2:1-4a) provides both closure to the unit as a whole and a pointer toward the rest of the Torah. It stands apart from the six days of creation, because God does not act or speak; God rests. The structuring of six plus one thus parallels the poetic device of X/X + 1 (e.g., Amos 1:3; Prov. 30:15-16, 18-19, 29-31). As the seven days of a week form a whole (six days of work and rest on the Sabbath), so do the units of creation; one provides the justification for the other. This conclusion parallels the introduction with the phrases: "the heavens and the earth," "create," and the contrast between "move" (1:2) and "rest" (2:2, 3). Genesis 2:4a, on the other hand, serves both as closure of the unit as well as anticipation of what happens within creation. For "these are the generations [or descendants or lineages]" is an introductory formula used twelve times through-out the Priestly materials in the Torah (see Gen. 5:1; 6:9; 10:1; 11:10, 27; 25:12, 19; 36:1, 9; 37:2; Num. 3:1).

In between the introduction and conclusion are the six days of creation. But rather than a completely symmetrical six acts of creation on six days, one finds eight acts of creation. This provides a different sort of symmetry: the double acts of creation occur on the third (dry land and vegetation) and sixth (land animals and humans) days. The recurring sequence (with varia-tions) is:

- Command (God speaks)
- Enactment (it happens according to God's word)
- Work (God makes, sets, separates)
- Empowerment (God blesses [creatures only])
- Evaluation/Affirmation (God sees that it is good)

And each day is concluded with the formula: "And there was evening and there was morning, day X." Thus creation is set off in seven daily seg-ments, with night and day; the world is separated into the skies, the land, and the seas; and the creatures are separated by their placement in the skies, the land, and the sea, with humans designated as a special class of land animal.

Exodus 34:4-6, 8-9. It is helpful to recapitulate the preceding narra-tives that lead up to this passage. The Decalog was first spoken by Yahweh to Moses (Exod. 20:1-17); and then he gave Moses two tablets "written by God's finger" (31:18). But when Moses descended the mountain and wit-nessed the Israelites worshiping the golden calf, he threw down the tablets and broke them (32:19). Yahweh then commanded Moses to make two new tablets and promised to write the same ten words on them (34:1). The odd thing is that at the end of the episode, the narrator leaves the reader in doubt whether it was Yahweh or Moses who wrote down the ten words (34:28b).

The proclamation of the divine name, Yahweh, highlights its sacral quality: just saying the name is a holy act (34:5). This name of Israel's God was always given special significance in the tradition. God appears to Moses in the burning bush (Exod. 3:13-16); and when Moses argues that he cannot appeal to the Israelites without knowing the name of this god, God replies with the cryptic threefold response: "I am who I am" (3:14a), "I am" (3:14b), and "Yahweh" (3:15a)—all forms of the verb "to be." Yah-weh then reveals that he is identical with "the God of Abraham, the God of Isaac, and the God of Jacob" (3:15b). In Exodus 6 a similar scene is played out. There Yahweh reveals the sacred name, and that he was known to the ancestors as "El Shaddai" (perhaps meaning "El of the mountains"). The protection of Yahweh's name is also part of the Decalog (20:7); but exactly what wrongful use of the divine name this would entail is not spelled out—perhaps using it in magical spells or swearing by Yahweh's name when one is knowingly lying.

Names are important in the ancient Mediterranean world for a number of reasons: (1) naming is an act of power, often defining character, relationship, or experience (see, e.g., Gen. 2:19-20; 25:24-26; 41:45); (2) in these honor/shame societies, one's name is a primary symbol of one's honor and reputation (see, e.g., Gen. 17:4-6; 2 Sam. 8:13); (3) knowing someone's name is a sign of intimacy and gives one power (see, e.g., Gen. 32:22-30); and (4) the presence of the divine name symbolizes God's cultic presence and thus can be successfully invoked (see, e.g., 1 Kgs. 8:27-30; Ps. 8:1).

What follows the proclamation of the name is a description of Yahweh passing in front of Moses and declaring a liturgical formula about Yahweh's character (vv. 6-7). It begins with a double pronouncement of the name and proceeds with a sequence of divine attributes: merciful, gracious, slow to anger, abounding in loyalty and faithfulness, keeping loyalty, and forgiving iniquity. That this is a liturgical formula is indicated by: (1) its poetic formulation; (2) its repetition in various forms throughout the tradition (see Exod. 33:19; Num. 14:18; 2 Chron. 30:9; Neh. 9:17, 31; Pss. 86:15; 103:8-9; 111:4; 145:8; Jer. 32:18; Joel 2:13; Jon. 4:2; Nah. 1:3a; Sir. 2:11; Man. 1:7); and (3) the ritual context of this passage: theophany (v. 5a), proclamation of the divine name (v. 5b), and Moses' response in prostration and worship (v. 8).

Deuteronomy 4 is the conclusion of the long introduction to the book (chaps. 1–4), setting up the reiteration of Yahweh's stipulations for living in the land (chaps. 5–26). The invitation in 4:32a is for Israel to ask regarding the incomparability of the experiences that they have had. The metaphors of completeness employed are, first, *temporal*—all the way back to the creation of the first human beings (v. 32a); and, second, *spatial*—from one end of the skies to the other (v. 32b). What follows are a series of four rhetorical questions that get increasingly longer—the first two general, and the second two specific:

- Has anything so great ever happened? (v. 32c)
- Has anything like this ever been heard of? (v. 32d)
- Has any people heard a divine voice . . . and lived? (v. 33)
- Has any god ever delivered a people from the midst of another people? (v. 34)

Just as Yahweh is incomparable (see Exod. 9:14; Isa. 44:7; Jer. 49:19), so is what Yahweh has accomplished in delivering Israel out of Egypt.

In vv. 39-40 Moses appeals to Israel to obey Yahweh's statutes out of community interest. Their obedience will lead to longevity in the land that Yahweh gives them, for themselves and their descendants. This landedness is an important theme in Deuteronomy precisely because the editors during the Babylonian exile know that they have been exiled from the land (see, e.g., Deut. 4:27-31; 28:41, 47-68; 30:4-10). The hope in this passage is that, given another chance, obedience will sustain them in the land.

The double use of the word *today* (Heb. *hayyôm*; "acknowledge today," v. 39; and "which I am commanding you today," v. 40) recalls the many times it is used throughout this book to emphasize the immediacy of the challenge set before the people (see, e.g., Deut. 1:39; 2:25; 4:8, 26; 5:1; 6:6; 7:11; 8:1, 11, 18, 19; 9:1, 3; 11:2, 8, 13, 27; 15:15; 30:2, 8; 31:27 [RSV]; 32:46). Once Moses' "day" has passed, Israel is still challenged in every generation by the call to obedience "today," as is clear in the reference to later generations.

SECOND LESSON: 2 CORINTHIANS 13:(5-10)11-14

Paul's Second Letter to the Corinthians is problematic in terms of its overall structure and composition. Many scholars believe it actually to be a compilation of letters and letter fragments that have been stitched together. If this is the case, the proposal has been that 10:1—13:13 is the "tearful letter" (or a fragment of it) referred to in 2 Cor. 2:3-4 and 7:8. The subject of this tearful letter is Paul's defense of his apostolic authority ("I will not be shamed," 10:8; and "we have been defending ourselves before you," 12:19) in the face of opponents. These opponents are self-styled "super-apostles" (11:5; 12:11), whom Paul calls "pseudo-apostles" (11:13); they have visions and revelations and seem to preach "a different Jesus" and "a different gospel" and possess "a different spirit" (11:4). Paul's listing of his "Israelite" credentials is in response to the super-apostles' claims of esteemed Israelite heritage (11:21-22), and, therefore, they are probably representative of "Judaizers" or the "circumcision party" mentioned elsewhere (e.g., Acts 11:2-3; Gal. 2:3-4, 11-12).

This passage provides the conclusion to 2 Corinthians as a whole. Verses 5-11a provide the closing exhortations (positive instructions) in quite general terms: "examine yourselves" (v. 5a); "test yourselves" (v. 5b); and "mend your ways, heed my appeal, agree with one another, live in peace" (v. 11a). But while the exhortations are general, the issues Paul reprises echo those addressed earlier in the letter: faith (v. 5; see 10:15), the truth (v. 8; see 11:10; 12:6), strength and weakness (v. 9; see 11:30; 12:5, 9-10), and apostolic authority (v. 10; see 10:8; 11:17). This is followed by the stereotypes of a Greek letter's conclusion: peace-wish (v. 11b; see 1 Thess. 5:23-24), exhorting a holy kiss (v. 12; see 1 Thess. 5:26), final greetings (v. 12b [RSV:13]; see 1 Cor. 16:19-20a), and a benediction (v. 13 [RSV:14]; see 1 Cor. 16:23-24).

GOSPEL: MATTHEW 28:16-20; JOHN 3:16-18

Matthew 28:16-20. The conclusion to Matthew's Gospel is Jesus' commissioning of the Eleven on a mountain in Galilee (Judas had previously hanged himself, 27:3-10). The reader's attention is drawn toward Galilee because the women to whom Jesus appeared at the tomb outside Jerusalem were commissioned to direct the Eleven to Galilee: both by the Lord's angel (28:7) and Jesus himself (28:10).

The postresurrection narratives display a wide diversity in the four canonical Gospels: in their number, contents, geographical settings, and characters. Mark's earliest ending (16:1-8) ends at the empty tomb outside Jerusalem with one young man in white commissioning the women to direct the Eleven to Galilee—but without an appearance of Jesus. Luke (chap. 24) keeps the action in and around Jerusalem (including Emmaus and Bethany), initiated by two men in dazzling clothes. John tells of both Jerusalem-area and Galilean encounters with the risen Jesus (John 20–21), including two angels in white: at the tomb, in locked rooms, and by the sea. In Matthew, Jesus also appears in both the Jerusalem area (28:9-10) and Galilee (28:16-20) after the women encounter an angel who descended from heaven (28:1-7). The number and identity of the women who encountered the messengers also varies from one Gospel to another: Mary Magdalene is mentioned in each account with various other female companions. The least one can conclude from these observations is that by the end of the first century different groups of Jesus followers had a variety of postresurrection traditions, and they were geographically centered in either the vicinity of Jerusalem (the location of Jesus' passion and burial), or Galilee (the location of his ministry and the base of his public support).

This commissioning scene in Matthew is remarkable for a number of reasons. First, the evangelist includes no dialog on the part of the disciples at this momentous meeting. This has the effect of placing all the attention on what Jesus says. Second, even in this account of a christophanic experience, the evangelist recounts division among the disciples: some worshiped, some doubted (v. 17)! This builds on a minor theme that runs throughout Matthew that the church is composed of both good and bad elements (see, e.g., 13:24-30, 36-43, 47-50; 22:1-14; 25:1-3). And third, Jesus surprisingly makes no comment upon the preceding events: his arrest, trial, crucifixion, and resurrection (26:1—28:10); Judas's betrayal and suicide (26:14-16, 47-56; 27:3-10); or Peter's threefold denial (26:69-75). It is as if all of these issues pale in contrast to the outwardly directed mission that Jesus now has for the disciples.

Why does the evangelist give this commissioning a mountain setting? It is important to see that this is the final mountain scene in this Gospel's sequence of five mountains. The earlier four are: the mountain of initiation (4:1-11 [8-11]), the mountain of instruction (5–7; see below on the Second Sunday after Pentecost, Matt. 7:15-29), the mountain of healing (15:29-31), and the mountain of epiphany (17:1-13). Mountains are important throughout the ancient Mediterranean and Middle Eastern world as locations of altars, temples, and other types of divine/human meeting. Mt. Sinai and Mt. Zion are especially significant mountains in Israelite and Judahite tradition as the loci where the Law is received by Moses and where Solomon builds the central Yahweh temple.

Mountains are the highest points, thus connecting earth and sky—the realms of the humans and God respectively. They take on symbolic significance as sacred meeting place and cosmic center. Their height is a multivalent symbol of reaching up toward the sky (and thus the divine world); prominence and honor symboled as "above," "high," or "over"; center of attention; distance from daily existence; danger (especially when volcanic); and inaccessibility (see Exod. 19:16-18). Isaiah captured several of these elements with reference to the Zion traditions:

> It shall happen in the latter days that the mountain of Yahweh's house shall be established as the highest of the mountains, and shall be raised above the hills; and all the nations shall flow to it, and many peoples shall come and say: "Come, let us go up to Yahweh's mountain, to the house of Jacob's God." (Isa. 2:2-3)

One can see the development of this symbolic significance of mountains in the book of Jubilees (part of the Judean Pseudepigrapha; 2nd cent. B.C.E.) which articulates the cosmic significance and relationship of Eden, Sinai, and Zion (*Jubilees* 8:19); and in *1 Enoch* (also in the Pseudepigrapha; 2nd cent. B.C.E.—1st cent. C.E.) one finds the connection of the navel of the earth, the cosmic tree, and the holy mountain (26:1).

What the evangelist signals to the audience is that something extraordinary will happen when Jesus goes "to the mountain" (his formulaic phrase). This extraordinary phenomenon is ritual transformation. None of the five mountains is named; so the significance is not placed on a particular location, but on the symbolic significance of the mountain. This is where the divine and humans meet; this is where transformation will take place. In each of these passages Jesus and those accompanying him are separated from the rest of society. Here in Matthew 28 the narrative begins with this separation and ascent of the mountain: "Now the eleven disciples went to Galilee, to the mountain to which Jesus had directed them" (v. 16). While on the mountain, Jesus commissions the disciples (vv. 18-20), transforming them from followers being trained to messengers with a mission. He also transforms them by broadening their audience from only reaching out "to the lost sheep of Israel" (10:6) to making "disciples of all peoples" (28:19). In the other mountain passages, Jesus descends the mountain and rejoins society. Here the evangelist allows the narrative to end with Jesus on the mountain with the disciples: no formal closure; no reaggregation of the transformed community. Instead, the closing sentence promises Jesus's ongoing presence, looking forward to "the end of the age" (v. 20).

The sequence of the mountains takes the audience through developmental stages of discipleship: initiation, teaching, healing, epiphany, and commissioning. So also does Matthew's mountain passage form a model of discipleship, one of the structuring principles of the Gospel, and a five-act ritual drama of Jesus's transforming presence.

John 3 begins with the dialog between Jesus and Nicodemus the Pharisee. The late-night visit is the first indication that Nicodemus belongs in the same category with Joseph of Arimathea: they are secret disciples (see John 19:38-39). The passage as a whole ends in 3:21, but it is unclear where the narrator intends the Jesus speech to end and the narration to resume; the last verse of Jesus' speech could be any verse from v. 12 to v. 21. The reason for the confusion is that in John the evangelist consistently obscures the difference between the voices of Jesus and the narrator.

The difficulty of reading these verses is that they have become so familiar that they are hard to hear afresh. The theme of love runs throughout the Gospel, but most of the time it refers to "in-group commitment":
- the Father's love for the Son (3:35; 5:20; 10:17; 15:9)
- the Son's love for the Father (14:31; 15:10)
- the Father's love for the disciples (16:27)
- Jesus' love for the disciples (13:1, 34; 15:9)
- the disciples' love for Jesus and the Father (14:15, 21-23)
- the disciples' love for one another (13:34-35; 15:12, 17).

Only in 3:16 does John say that God loves the "world" (Gk. *kosmos*); the closest parallel is that whoever hears and believes has eternal life (5:24). The statement in John 3:16 is so startling because most of the time in John "the cosmos" is not a neutral term: it is the hostile society that rejects the Son (see, e.g., 1:10; 7:7; 8:23; 14:17; 15:18-19; 17:9).

It is important that the Son's mission is not condemnation, but deliverance. This word is most often translated as "salvation," but in Western societies salvation has come to have such individualistic, interior, and solely "spiritual" connotations. Both in Hebrew (yaša') and Greek (sôzô), "to deliver" relates to a variety of contexts: economic, military, health, life, safety, exorcism of demons. The deliverance that Jesus mediates is much broader and deeper than "saving souls"; he delivers whole persons from the brink of whatever precipice they stand.

HOMILETICAL CONSIDERATIONS

While the account in Genesis 1 dominates how many people think of "biblical" creation, in fact the Bible includes a panoply of ways of talking about the creation of the world. No one metaphor exhausts the complexity and enormity of God's creative acts, and a sampling of these provides a sense of the diversity in the tradition; the sense of wonder could not be elicited by one expression, one set of metaphors, one vision:

• Like Genesis 1, Ps. 33:6 notes that Yahweh creates by his word.

• In Gen. 2:4b-25 Yahweh creates the first human by fashioning it/him out of clay or dust, and continues by developing the earth like a gardener.

• In Isa. 51:9-12 the prophet combines creation and Exodus motifs, describing a swordfight of Yahweh against Rahab and Leviathan, the last two being names of traditional chaos "dragons."

• In order to shame Job and contrast divine with human power, Yahweh employs a variety of images for creative acts and control over creation in Job 38: builder (vv. 4-7), seamstress (v. 9), irrigation-channel digger (vv. 25-27), father and mother (vv. 28-29), and wild animal trainer and feeder (vv. 31-33, 39-41).

• In wisdom texts (including the Apocrypha), God is either assisted by Woman Wisdom (Heb. *Chokmah*; Gk. *Sophia*) or creates through her. In Prov. 8:22-31, Woman Wisdom is the first of all created, and she assists like a "site manager." In Wisd. 8:6, she is described as the one who fashioned all things. Playing on this tradition, John 1:1-3 describes the divine Logos/Jesus as the mediator of creation (see also Col. 1:15-20; Heb. 1:2).

Whatever the metaphor or image, all these biblical texts understand Yahweh, the God of Israel, to be the source of the whole creation. The universe is not the result of random chance, nor the act of some human. It is spoken, built, sewn, or fashioned into shape by a power beyond human control or comprehension.

Despite popular conceptions of creation, the notion of *creatio ex nihilo* ("creation from nothing") was a very late development in Judahite theology. The first text of the Bible that might point toward this view is in the Apocrypha: "I beg you, my child, to look at the heaven and the earth and see everything that is in them, and recognize that God did not make them out of things that already existed" (2 Macc. 7:28). Genesis 1:1—2:4a speaks not to creation from nothing, but *order out of chaos.* And this indicates the focus of creation language in the biblical tradition; for it does not address the question of from where all the molecules and atoms come, but God's ability to bring shape and substance out of shapelessness and emptiness. This is the ongoing significance of God's creation: God creates community, harmony, structure, and orderliness. Human greed, jealousy, hatred, and selfishness generate chaos and destruction. To view the world through the eyes of faith is to see God's empowerment of the universe: to manifest its goodness, to reproduce, to fill it with life. As G. K. Chesterton wrote: "The world will never starve for wonders; but only for want of wonder."

Second Sunday after Pentecost
Ninth Sunday in Ordinary Time
Proper 5

Lectionary	First Lesson	Psalm	Second Lesson	Gospel
Revised Common	Hosea 5:15—6:6	Ps. 50:7-15	Rom. 4:13-25	Matt. 9:9-13, 18-26
Episcopal (BCP)	Hosea 5:15—6:6	Psalm 50 or 50:7-15	Rom. 4:13-18	Matt. 9:9-13
Roman Catholic	Deut. 11:18, 26-28, 32	Ps. 31:2-4, 17, 25	Rom. 3:21-25a, 28	Matt. 7:21-27
Lutheran (LBW)	Deut. 11:18-21, 26-28	Ps. 31:1-5 (6-18), 19-24	Rom. 3:21-25a, 27-28	Matt. 7: (15-20), 21-29

FIRST LESSON: DEUTERONOMY 11:18-21, 26-28; HOSEA 5:15—6:6

Deuteronomy 11:18-21, 26-28. Long-term relationships are difficult to sustain. As human beings, we are easily distracted or diverted; our attention spans can be frustratingly brief; our interest may wax and wane. The human relationship with God is no different. This is recognized from the earliest parts of the biblical tradition: promises, oaths, contracts, and covenants all speak to the necessity of creating structures and formal parameters for entering into commitments with others. If we, as humans, have spiritual Attention Deficit Disorder, these are means of addressing our handicap.

This passage follows the giving of the Decalog (Ten Commandments) for the second time (10:1-5), and concludes a long, rather repetitive, section that drives home the point of allegiance to Yahweh, Israel's patron-god. Most of this is in very general language: obeying all that Yahweh commands; serving, fearing, worshiping, and loving Yahweh; and "circumcising" their hearts. But *how* will Israel remember to do all this? That is the focus of this passage. The simple structure of vv. 18-21 is:

> I. Series of instructions: handling Yahweh's words (18-20)
>> A. Put (18a)
>>> 1. In one's heart (18a1)
>>> 2. In one's life/soul (18a2)
>> B. Bind on hand (18b)
>> C. Fix between eyes (18c)
>> D. Teach to children (19)
>>> 1. When sitting and walking (19a)
>>> 2. When lying down and rising up (19b)
>> E. Write (20)
>>> 1. On doorposts (20a)
>>> 2. On gateposts (20b)
> II. Consequence: multiplied days in the land (21)

In the series of instructions, the audience is given a sequence of binary oppositions. In v. 18 Israel is instructed that Yahweh's words shall be both internalized (heart and life [soul]) and externalized (on the hand and between the eyes). The hand symbolizes purposeful action, one's deeds, and the head symbolizes emotion-fused thought; a unity of word and deed connects the two parts. In vv. 19 and 20 Israel is instructed that the perpetuation of Yahweh's words should take place orally (teaching, v. 19) and in writing (v. 20). The teaching should occur both inside ("sitting in your house") and outside ("when you are walking on the road"), in the evening ("when you lie down") and in the morning ("when you rise"). And the writing should appear at the entryways to the house ("on your doorposts") and the entryways to the village/city ("on your gates"). These binary pairs cover the community's life: inside/outside, word/deed, oral/written, night/day, home/village. Commitment and memory, therefore, enter into every aspect of life: wherever one goes, Yahweh's words permeate the community's experience.

The physical binding on the hand and between the eyes developed in later Judahite tradition in the use of phylacteries (Aramaic *tepillin*; leather or wooden boxes, containing the commandments, strapped to the body with leather thongs; see Matt. 23:5). The four traditional biblical passages included inside phylacteries are Exod. 13:1-10, 11-16; Deut. 6:4-9; 11:13-21; but the phylacteries discovered at Qumran additionally included the Decalog. The posting at doorways took shape in the *mezuzah* (the biblical passages in a container fastened to the doorpost).

The consequence of maintaining commitment to these instructions (and, therefore, commitment to Yahweh) is longevity in the land. Here Deuteronomy connects these instructions to the covenants with Abraham: to have numerous descendants (Gen. 12:2; 15:4-6; 17:2-7) and possession of Canaan (Gen. 15:7, 18-21; 17:8). Thus, even though the Decalog is not narrative, it functions as a thematic bridge between the patriarchal sagas in Genesis and the conquest of Canaan in Joshua.

But the land is understood as gift. Deuteronomy is cognizant of the effects of disobedience, and provides an interpretation of the Babylonian exile (598–540 B.C.E.) as the ultimate punishment for infidelity (e.g., Deut. 4:27-31; 28:41, 47-68; 30:4-10). All the material in Deuteronomy does not originate in the exile, but that is when it most likely went through its final editing. So the relationship of the people to the land is of fundamental significance to the audience.

After a section on driving out Israel's enemies from the land (11:22-25), the passage continues the binary oppositions with reference to the blessing and curse in relation to obedience and disobedience (11:26-28). In modern, technological societies such as the United States, talk of blessing and curse carries little weight or interest. The pastor's blessing at the end of Christian worship services often functions simply at the level of "closing words." But in traditional societies, such as ancient Israel, these bore great import. Blessing and curse are *words of power*, not simply wishing someone well or ill (see Num. 22:6). Therefore, it is always either God (e.g., Gen. 1:28; 3:14-15) or a broker of God's power—priest (e.g., Num. 6:22-27), king (e.g., 2 Sam. 6:18), or clan-leader (e.g., Gen. 27:18-29)—who is in a position to bless or curse. For a curse ritual, see Deut. 27:11-26; for a blessing ritual, see Deut. 33:1-29.

The "Community Rule" from Qumran provides a good example of the coupling of blessing and curse in a ritual setting; the priestly blessing of the faithful (in this case, those who join the community) is coupled with the levitical curse of the wicked (those who do not join):

> And the priests shall pronounce a blessing on all the men who have cast their lot with God—those who walk in integrity in all their ways and say:
>> "May he bless you with all goodness,
>> and protect you from all evil,
>> and illuminate your heart with the insight of life,
>> and bestow on you knowledge of eternal matters;
>> and may he raise his loyal face toward you for eternal peace."
>
> And the Levites shall pronounce a curse on all the men who have cast their lot with Belial and respond and say:
>> "Cursed are you in all your wickedly evil deeds.
>> May God make you accursed in the hand of all who take vengeance,
>> and assign your descendants to destruction
>> at the hand of all who exact reprisals.
>> Cursed are you! Hopeless!
>> Like the darkness are your deeds.
>> Denounced are you into the gloom of perpetual fire.
>> May God neither be gracious to you when you cry out,
>> nor forgive for the purification of your sins.
>> May he raise his face to wreak vengeance on you.
>> And may none of those who possesses their patrimony say to you: 'Peace.'"
>
> And all that enter into the covenant shall respond after the pronouncements of the blessing and curse: "Amen, Amen." (1QS 2.1-10; my translation)

Hosea 5:15—6:6. The superscription to the whole book of Hosea places the prophet's activities in the mid- to late-eighth century B.C.E. (1:1); and his focus of attention was the northern kingdom of Israel, indicated by Samaria, Ephraim, and Israel (see, e.g., 7:1; 10:5; 13:9, 16). This puts

Hosea in the same period with Amos in Israel, and Isaiah and Micah in Judah. The Assyrians, led by Tiglath-pileser III, were a major threat in this era, expanding their political-military-economic control westward. Circa 738 B.C.E. the Israelite king, Menachem, submitted to Assyrian hegemony and paid a steep tribute (2 Kgs. 15:19-20). But for the next two decades Israel vacillated between paying Assyrian tribute and looking to Egypt and other neighbors for protection (see Hos. 7:11). In 735–733 B.C.E. the Syro-Ephraimite War was fought between the anti-Assyrian coalition (including Israel) against Judah (2 Kgs. 16:5-9). And finally in 721 the Assyrians, led by Sargon II, invaded Israel and destroyed Samaria (2 Kgs. 17:1-41). Hosea 4–8 form a thematic section of prophecies on Israel's unfaithfulness and disloyalty.

The passage begins with Yahweh speaking the disheartening word that he is departing Israel until the people are ready to repent and "seek my face" (5:15). This image of Yahweh's departure is reflected in Ezekiel: The prophet has a vision of Yahweh ordering the defilement of the Jerusalem temple, followed by Yahweh's glory departing from the temple and then the city (Ezek. 9:3—10:19; 11:22-25). The departure of Yahweh's presence speaks to a broken relationship, a breakdown of communication, and a sense of distance. These are the negative flip side of seeking Yahweh's face.

The hopeful section that follows in 6:1-3 can be read in at least two different ways. On the one hand, it can be read straightforwardly as the prophet's articulation of what a contrite liturgy of repentance should sound like. On the other hand, however, the larger context of ridicule and chastisement may lead to a reading of this as a parody of Israel's repentance. It is immediately followed by a comparison of Israel and Judah's commitment to a wispy morning cloud or dew, which evaporates so quickly (6:4). That is, the beauty of imagery in the liturgy is contrasted with the shallowness of relationship exhibited by the people.

The sharp critique of sacrifices and burnt offerings in v. 6 sounds especially attractive to Christian ears (see, e.g., Heb. 10:1-18). It certainly has echoes both in other prophetic books and the Psalms (Ps. 40:6-8; 50:8-15; 51:16-19; Isa. 1:10-17; Jer. 6:20; 7:21-26; Amos 5:21-24; Mic. 6:6-8). What underlies all of these attacks on sacrifice and temple ritual is the lack of social integrity. The people are accused of participating in all the rites, but failing to manifest God's character in their communities. One might also say that the sacrifices and rituals are meant to give concrete expression to the relationship between Israel and Yahweh; but these prophets accuse Israel of substituting the rituals for a relationship of integrity. If Yahweh is a God of grace and mercy, the question becomes, Where is that manifested in the society? (See below on Matt. 9:9-13, 18-26.)

PSALM 31

This is an individual complaint psalm crying out for Yahweh's help (see also Psalms 6; 7; 13; 16; 17; 22; 28; see below on the Fourth Sunday after Pentecost, Jer. 20:7-13 and Psalm 69). The characteristic petitions in imperatives and related forms identify what the psalmist wants from Yahweh: never let me be put to shame (vv. 1a, 17a), extricate (v. 1b), incline (v. 2a), rescue (v. 2b, 15b), be a rock and fortress (v. 2c-d), lead and guide (v. 3b), take out (v. 4a), be gracious (v. 9), deliver (v. 16b), let . . . be shamed (v. 17c), let go (v. 17d), let be . . . dumb (v. 18a).

The song shifts back and forth between these cries for help and expressions of confidence, as if deliverance has already been accomplished. After "you have ransomed me" (v. 5b), an extended note of triumph is sung:

> you have seen my affliction;
> you have taken notice of my adversities,
> and have not delivered me up into my enemy's hands;
> you have set my feet in a spacious place. (vv. 7-8)

But this is immediately followed with more cries of distress (vv. 9-13). Indeed, the psalmist is "like the dead" (v. 12a) and there is "terror on every side" (v. 13a). So the triumph in vv. 7-8 should be read as anticipatory.

At the end, however, Yahweh seems to have successfully defeated the terror. As in traditional songs of thanksgiving, the psalmist quotes his earlier complaints (see Pss. 30:2-3, 8-10; 116:4, 10-11), and identifies them as heard and answered (vv. 21-22). The conclusion is a call to love Yahweh (v. 23a), followed by another affirmation of confidence (v. 23b-c).

The theology of these songs of complaint is focused upon Yahweh's ability and willingness to act on behalf of the afflicted. Yahweh is a "rock and fortress" (v. 3a), a "refuge" (v. 4b), a "God of faithfulness" (v. 5b), a God of "loyalty" (Heb. *chesed*, vv. 7, 16, 21). But, foundational to the whole relationship, Yahweh is one who sees, listens, and knows (vv. 2a, 7b-c, 22c).

SECOND LESSON: ROMANS 3:21-25,27-28; 4:13-25

Since the epistle lessons for the next several weeks are from Paul's Letter to the Romans, it may be helpful to make some introductory remarks here about the epistle as a whole. Romans is one of the "undisputed" Pauline epistles, along with 1 Thessalonians, 1 Corinthians, 2 Corinthians, Philippians, Philemon, and Galatians. Those commonly identified as "deutero-Pauline" (secondary) seem to stem from circles of those influenced by Paul, often writing in his name: 2 Thessalonians, Colossians, Ephesians, 1 Timothy, 2 Timothy, and Titus. The bases for this distinction are differences in vocabulary, style, theology, and perspectives on church organization. The letter was written (perhaps from Corinth? see 15:25-26) in the period of 54–58 C.E. to an established congregation in Rome. It is clear that Paul did not begin this congregation, and that he had no firsthand knowledge of it (1:10, 13, 15; 15:22-23). It is also evident that the congregation was composed predominantly of gentile Christians (see, e.g., 1:13-14; 11:13-16; 15:15-21).

The structure of the letter follows (for the most part) the classical style of Hellenistic epistles:

I. Introduction	1:1-17
A. Salutation	1:1-7
1. Sender: Paul	1:1-6
2. Recipients: "saints" in Rome	1:7a
3. Greeting	1:7b
B. Thanksgiving	1:8-17
II. Central Section	1:18—15:32
A. Body	1:18—11:36
1. Justification through faith	1:18—4:25
2. New life in Christ	5:1—8:39
3. Israel in God's plan	9:1—11:36
B. Ethical Instruction	12:1—15:32
III. Conclusion	15:33—16:27
A. Peace Wish	15:33
B. Commendation: Phoebe	16:1-2
C. Greetings from Paul to 26 individuals & 2 families	16:3-15
D. Exhortation of "holy kiss"	16:16
E. Concluding exhortation	16:17-20a
F. Benediction	16:20b
G. Greetings from 8 of Paul's associates	16:21-23
H. Doxology	16:25-27

Several observations should be made concerning the structure. First, note the unusually extended self-identification of the sender (1:1-6). Normally, this would only cite the sender's name, or perhaps an additional phrase or two. Here, Paul extends his identification into a virtual summary of, not only his apostleship, but his understanding of the gospel. This may be explained by the fact that Paul had never been to Rome, and thus he used this literary flourish to introduce himself. Second, many scholars believe Romans 16 is a separate letter that has been "tacked on" to the end of Romans 1–15. This letter's conclusion is more complex than those in Paul's other letters; it includes a recommendation (16:1-2), two sets of greetings, and an extensive doxology. Paul's own greetings (vv. 3-13) are separated from the greetings of his companions and scribe (vv. 21-23). The recommendation is unique in Paul's letters, as is the doxology as a letter's conclusion (but brief doxologies do appear in both the Pauline and deutero-Pauline epistles; see, e.g., Rom. 11:36; Gal. 1:5; Eph. 3:20-21; Phil. 4:20; 1 Tim. 1:17; 6:15b-16; 2 Tim. 4:18b). A further problem with the doxology is that the earliest Greek manuscripts signal its problematic status; in some it appears at the end of chapter 16, in others it does not appear at all, and in others it is found at the end of either chapter 14 or 15.

This passage in **Romans 3:21-31, 27-28** is a compressed articulation of Paul's most important theological themes: God's righteousness, Christ's death, justification by faith, sin, works, the law, and the relationship of Judeans and Gentiles, developing the formulations in 1:16-17. It appears as a summary and transition passage in Paul's larger argument (1:18—11:36), and at the center of the first section (1:18—4:25), where Paul outlines his understanding of sin and God's judgment of Judeans and Gentiles. In 4:1-25 Paul discusses Abraham as model of faith, providing a basis in Scripture for his argument. Romans 3:21-31, then, summarizes the argument up to this point.

The argument may be clearer if we break it down into its component parts:

1. God is righteous (acts faithfully in God's role as patron) (3:21, 22, 25, 26);
2. all peoples are alienated from God due to "sin" (missing the mark) (3:23);
3. God does not discriminate between Judeans and Gentiles (crossing traditional Judean purity lines expressed in the Law and Prophets) (3:22, 23, 29-30);
4. God's part of the relationship is graciously giving Christ and forbearing sin (3:24-25);
5. God's declaration of restored relationship and "redemption" (buying out of slavery) is manifested through Jesus' death (3:24-25);
6. the human part of the relationship is expressed in "faith" (loyalty and commitment) (3:22, 25-28, 30-31);
7. "works of the law" (compliance with traditional Israelite norms: the Law) are incapable of accomplishing justification (3:27-28, 31).

In order to track the logic of such a passage one needs first to understand that it is rhetorical argument operating at a highly abstract level, accessing a complex set of symbols. Paul juxtaposes metaphors drawn from a variety of sources (temple sacrifice, law, patron-client relationships) and brings them together in his rhetorical argument. His point is to argue for the possibility of new relationship between God and humans, not based upon performance of legal responsibilities or social custom, but on gift and loyalty. The facilitator of this new arrangement is Jesus, by means of his death.

What does Paul affirm about God in this key passage? First, "righteousness" (Gk. *dikaiosynê*) is central. The phrase "God's (or: his) righteousness" appears in vv. 21, 22, 25; and the adjective "righteous" (*dikaios*) and verb "make righteous" (or "justify"; *dikaioô*) also appear with God as the subject in vv. 24, 26, 28, 30. Righteousness is a highly debated term among Pauline scholars, but I would agree with those who understand it as a relational term, in this case between a "patron" (God) and "clients" (humans). The "broker" in this relationship is Jesus. God's righteousness, then, is the honorable upholding of the role of patron; to make humans righteous is to put us in proper relationship, which is a gracious gift (v. 24). (The other major interpretation of righteousness is to take it as a term of legal standing.)

The second theological affirmation is that "God is one" (v. 30). For Paul, this relates, not simply to monotheism, but to God's singular mode of treating humans: impartiality toward and equal treatment of Judeans and Gentiles (vv. 22-23, 29-30). Because God is unified, God deals with humanity in a fair and unified way. And third, God's unity and righteousness are manifested in concrete ways: gracious giving (v. 24) and forbearance (or patience) toward sin (v. 25).

Romans 4:13-25. In this part of Paul's argument on the function of justification by faith, he hearkens back to the Israelite Torah—not to the legislations, but to the so-called "patriarchal" traditions, specifically to the stories of God's promises to Abraham and Abraham's responses (Gen. 12:2; 15:1-21; 17:1-21; and 22:1-19). The central question addressed is, Why did God "reckon" Abraham righteous?

It is fundamental to Paul's argument here that one sees that the initiative is always God's: God promises land and heirs (v. 13), raises the dead (v. 17), creates (v. 17), and makes righteous (vv. 22-25). Abraham's response to God is what Paul calls upon his readers to emulate: he believed (v. 18), he did not weaken in loyalty (v. 19), and he did not waver (v. 20). Note also Paul's exaggeration in v. 13 that God promised Abraham's heirs "the world" (Gk. *kosmos*), rather than land (compare Gen. 17:8)!

Paul moves from the example of Abraham to its relevance for his readers. He begins with the metaphorical transfer of Abraham's "heirs," from the literal descendants of his line (v. 13) to the metaphor of all who share in Abraham's faith (v. 16). In other words, Paul employs Abraham here not simply because he acted faithfully; presumably many in the biblical accounts would fit that profile. But Abraham is especially appropriate for Paul's argument because the promises to Abraham narratively precede the giving of the laws to Moses recorded in Exodus to Numbers. This, then, allows Paul to make Abraham the "father" of all the faithful, whether Judean or Gentile, and therefore to present another metaphor for fictive kinship ("families" not constructed on the basis of birth or marriage) so vital to his inclusive agenda. Paul, also, at least implies a parallel between the seemingly hopeless situations of Abraham and Sarah's advanced age and barrenness to Jesus' death: God was able to breath life and hope into both situations.

GOSPEL: MATTHEW 7:(15-20) 21-29; 9:9-13, 18-26

Matthew 7:(15-20) 21-29. This series of sayings forms the conclusion to the Sermon on the Mount (Matthew 5–7). The "Sermon" provides the second of Matthew's five ritual transformations on mountain tops (see above on the First Sunday after Pentecost, Matt. 28:16-18). To begin the transformation, the separation is recounted with the crowds following Jesus from the major Palestinian regions (4:25): Galilee (north), Decapolis (northeast), Jerusalem and Judea (south), and "beyond the Jordan" (southeast). This crowd gathering speaks to two issues: Jesus' increasing honor, and his increased honor as a source of envy for the Judean leaders (see 26:3-5). Jesus then went "to the mountain" (the identifying formula in these passages; see Matt. 4:8; 15:29; 17:1; 28:16). This is paralleled with his rejoining the main body of society (and sometimes descent) in four of the passages (4:12; 8:1; 15:39; 17:9, 14). The commissioning ends with Jesus and the disciples still on the mountain, pointing to "the end of the age" (28:20). What happens on these five mountains is a succession of ritual transformations: (1) Jesus is initiated as prophet, (2) the crowd is given instruction, (3) the crowd is healed, (4) Jesus' inner circle has an epiphanic experience, (5) and the Eleven are transformed from the followers/disciples of Jesus to a outwardly directed mission.

It is only in Matthew one finds the mountains as settings for transformational experiences of God's reign. And these unnamed mountains number five (note that Matthew also has five major discourses), probably to play into the theme of Jesus as "the new Moses" (five books in the Torah, and Moses' repeated trips to Mt. Sinai). Thus these mountains have taken on symbolic significance as an extraordinary setting for extraordinary events. Here the crowd is transformed by Jesus' foundational proclamation of God's reign, with the evangelist gathering sayings from all over his two basic sources (Mark and Q, the sayings source) along with unique materials. What the evangelist encodes in these narrative settings by cuing the reader to ritual is that two key things happen on the mountains: relationality and transformation. And both the relationality and transformation narrated in Jesus' ministry are manifestations of God's fatherhood and reign at work.

The whole conclusion to the "Sermon on the Mount" is 7:13-29. Each of these final sayings deals with in-group/out-group issues. The five sayings that precede the narrative conclusion are arranged in the following manner:

1. Contrast of narrow and wide gates (vv. 13-14//Luke 13:23-24);
2. Contrast of outward appearance and inward reality (v. 15; no parallel);
3. Contrast of good and bad trees (vv. 16-20//Luke 6:43-45);
4. Contrast of saying and doing (vv. 21-23//Luke 6:46);
5. Contrast of wise and foolish builders (vv. 24-27//Luke 6:47-49).

(The second and third sayings were originally independent of one another; but the evangelist has used the latter to explain and expand upon the former.) The type of binary contrasts found in this section is typical of ancient Middle Eastern discourse. Value judgments (especially as they relate to group definition) are often symbolized in binary oppositions, for example: light/dark (Matt. 6:22-23), love/hate (Matt. 6:24), acknowledge/deny (Matt. 10:32-33), for/against (Matt. 12:30), inside/outside (Matt. 23:25-26), right/left (Matt. 25:32-33), and above/below (John 8:23). So in Proverbs, for example, the recurring contrasts of characters and character traits are: wise/fool, righteous/wicked, rich/poor, arrogant/humble, upright/ treacherous, good/evil.

The first and fifth sayings employ metaphors for the difficult path of discipleship: the challenge of squeezing through a narrow gate and having the superior sense to build upon a solid foundation. Along with group identity issues (who is really in the group?), the second, third, and fourth sayings address the issue of *discernment* in the community (how can one recognize the true from the false?). These sayings emphasize that one may be misled by appearances and words. But the answer to this potential confusion is to focus on outcomes—in Matthew's terminology "fruits" (Gk. *karpos*, v. 20).

Fruit is one of the evangelist's recurring themes: disciples of Jesus manifest their in-group status through observable results: "fruit of repentance" (Matt. 3:8), "good fruit/bad fruit" (3:10; 12:33), "no fruit" (21:19), "season of fruit" (21:34, 41), and "producing the fruits" (21:43). These images of fruit recall Paul's list of the fruit of the Spirit: "love, joy, peace, patience, kindness, generosity, faithfulness, gentleness, and self-control" (Gal. 5:22-23). Matthew's highlighting Jesus' use of the fruit metaphor emphasizes for disciples the connection of ends and means, external manifestations of internal substance, and the integrity of word and deed.

But it is doubtful that the evangelist understands these sayings as simply good ideas to keep in mind. Since this climax of the "Sermon" focuses so clearly on in-group/out-group issues, one may conclude that group definition was a key issue for the evangelist and the group/s which he addressed. This speaks to conditions of uncertainty concerning who is truly a member of the group, and, perhaps, competition between early groups of Jesus followers. The naive might be easily deceived about the boundaries, these sayings indicate, but they need to focus attention on the integration of speech and action, manifestation of wisdom, and a recognition of the hazards of discipleship.

Matthew 9:9-13, 18-26. The evangelist provides few geographical cues in the Gospel for the reader, but this section is set around the perimeter of the Sea of Galilee. Matthew 9:1 indicates that Jesus had returned in a boat from Gadara (8:28) and arrived "at his own town" (for this expression, see 4:13), referring to Capernaum (Gk. *Caphernaoum*, meaning "village of Nahum") located on the northwest coast of the sea.

The call of Matthew in 9:9 is as simple and straightforward as a narrative could be. But even this brief account raises perplexing questions. While the disciple is identified as Matthew here, in the parallel accounts Mark calls the toll collector "Levi, the son of Alphaeus" (Mark 2:14), while Luke refers to him as simply "Levi" (Luke 5:27-28). This is further confused by the fact that in listing the names of the Twelve, all the Gospels and Acts designate James (the English form of "Jacob") as the "son of Alphaeus," rather than Matthew (Matt. 10:3; Mark 3:18; Luke 6:15; Acts 1:13).

Were "Matthew" and "Levi" two names for the same person? Was "Matthew" substituted for "Levi" so as to have the call narrative refer to one of the Twelve, when it originally was about an otherwise unknown disciple? Who was/were the son/s of Alphaeus: Levi, James, both? Was the name "Matthew" (Gk. *Maththaios* or *Matthaios*) chosen here because it provides a nice play on the Greek word for disciples (*mathêtai*)? If that is so, this call narrative could symbolically refer to all disciples, or to Matthew as the archetypal disciple. In all likelihood, the evangelist has substituted "Matthew" for "Levi" as an adaptation of the tradition from Mark in order to highlight the theme of discipleship (for further argument and documentation, see Dennis C. Duling, "Matthew [Disciple]" in *Anchor Bible Dictionary*, 4:618-22).

Two things are striking about the call itself. The first is that the two-word call/invitation ("Follow me") is followed by a similarly succinct compliance report ("And he arose and followed him"). The directness and brevity are startling, not because the scene is therefore difficult to follow, but because the simplicity of speech and action contrasts with the enormity of the implications for the disciple: leaving one's social grouping (family, village, friends, guild) in order to follow Jesus. "Follow me" is the recurring formula in the Gospels as the formal call to discipleship, and Matthew uses it more than Mark or Luke (see Matt. 4:19; 8:22; 9:9; 10:38; 16:24; 19:21). And from the literary contexts, most of the other uses of "follow" (Gk. *akoloutheô*) in relation to Jesus point to following in discipleship rather than simply tagging along (see Matt. 4:20, 22, 25; 8:1, 10, 19; 12:15; 14:13; 19:2, 27, 28; 20:29, 34; 27:55).

The implications of the call are linked to the second issue: Jesus is calling this disciple from the toll collector's booth! A toll collector (Gk. *telônês*) at Capernaum might be collecting tolls or other indirect taxes on merchandise transported across the sea, or on goods transported on the road which follows the western seaboard of the Sea of Galilee, or regulating the fishing on the sea. What is astonishing about Jesus calling a disciple from such an occupation is indicated by the hostility this drew from those who resented Roman occupation and rule by Roman clients (9:10-11). Direct taxes (e.g., poll tax and land tax), tolls (e.g., on roads, bridges, transport, leases, merchandise), and tribute (provincial debt to the Roman Empire) were not levied for the benefit of the population, as is the goal in modern, Western-style democracies. They were levied for the benefit of the Roman emperor, his clients, the Herodian rulers, and the Jerusalem elite. In short, the political economy of ancient Judea and Galilee can be characterized as "extractive" or "tributary"; that is, it was an economy that flowed away from the general peasant population toward the urban elites. Any improvements that the Romans made (e.g., aqueducts and paved roads) were done to benefit the urban elite, make the fiscal extraction more efficient, or facilitate Roman troop movement. Toll collectors may have been small cogs in the Roman wheel, probably hirelings of a wealthy chief toll collector (Gk. *architelônês*; see Luke 19:2). But it is clear in the sources that they put themselves in a difficult social position because: (1) they participated in the Roman imperial tax system; and (2) they had to come into direct contact with people and goods that were "unclean." They could easily be linked with the socially reprehensible position of prostitutes (see Matt. 21:31-32), adulterers, extortionists, and the "dishonorable" (see Luke 18:11).

This view of toll collectors, then, explains the Pharisees' outrage. The phrase "toll collectors and sinners" (9:10) has long been disputed because of the ambiguity of "sinners"; three possibilities emerge. First, it may simply be a double reference to the toll collectors. Second, "sinners" may refer to anyone who would associate with a toll collector. Or third, it may refer to the common people ("the people of the land") who did not adhere to the strict standards of the Pharisees ("the righteous"), who wanted all the people to abide by priestly levels of purity. Whichever was the case, Jesus' response demonstrates that their purity codes which kept them separate from outsiders was counterproductive to his agenda. He came to reach out to those who had been negatively labelled and excluded (9:13). Quoting from Hos. 6:6 (LXX), Jesus places the emphasis on mercy (see above, Hos. 5:15—6:6).

HOMILETICAL CONSIDERATIONS

Christians need to be just as attentive as ancient Israel to the integrity of worship and ethics, and to the connection of vertical and horizontal relationships (Hos. 6:6). Ethical considerations certainly emerge as important issues in Matthew 7, especially as they relate to group definition: who we are is manifested in how we live. But the passages from Romans and Matthew 9 are fundamental reminders of how ethics are meant to be manifested in Christian life. They are first of all the result of invitation ("Follow me") and relationship; and that relationship is fundamentally loyalty and trust (Hos. 6:4-6; Rom. 3:28).

But the good news, as articulated by Paul, is that no amount of performance can put us in right relationship with God; that is as simple and as complex as a gift—only grace is strong enough to accomplish that (Rom. 3:24). The "purity codes," such as those that Jesus' opponents were so anxious to protect (Matt. 9:11), often frustrate God's reaching out to us in our brokenness and need. The "rules" can never become more important than the people who need love, both God's and ours. The rules sometimes provide the comfort of clarity, but often they are barriers, shackles, and straitjackets.

Third Sunday after Pentecost
Tenth Sunday in Ordinary Time
Proper 6

Lectionary	First Lesson	Psalm	Second Lesson	Gospel
Revised Common	Exod. 19:2-8a	Psalm 100	Rom. 5:1-8	Matt. 9:35—10:8 (9-23)
Episcopal (BCP)	Exod. 19:2-8a	Psalm 100	Rom. 5:6-11	Matt. 9:35—10:8 (9-15)
Roman Catholic	Hosea 6:3-6	Ps. 50;1, 8, 12-15	Rom. 4:18-25	Matt. 9:9-13
Lutheran (LBW)	Hosea 5:15—6:6	Ps. 50:1-15	Rom. 4:18-25	Matt. 9:9-13

FIRST LESSON: EXODUS 19:2-8A

Following the plagues and the escape from Egypt by way of the sea, the Israelites finally arrive at the mountain in the Sinai wilderness (it is not called Mt. Sinai here). In line with ancient Mediterranean and Middle Eastern tradition, the mountain serves as an appropriate meeting place for deity and humans (note the later importance of Mt. Zion in Judah and Mt. Gerezim in Samaria). For example, referring to the number and variety of Israel's shrines, Yahweh says to Jeremiah: "Have you seen what she did, that faithless one, Israel, how she went up on every high hill and under every green tree, and played the whore there?" (Jer. 3:6).

Furthermore, the ancient gods were often described as living on mountains (e.g., Zeus on Olympus, Baal on Zaphon, Apollo on Parnassus). This is probably connected to the image of the mountain as highest point, separate from human society, a pinnacle, prominent, an honorable place, the "navel of the world" (see Judg. 9:37). While a minor motif in Old Testament literature, the mountain's cosmic symbolism is elaborated in later Judean literature. In *Jubilees* (c. second cent. B.C.E.) one reads:

> And he knew that the garden of Eden was the holy of holies and the dwelling of the LORD. And Mount Sinai [was] in the midst of the desert and Mount Zion [was] in the midst of the navel of the earth. The three of them were created as holy places, one facing the other (8:19).

In *1 Enoch* one finds the connection of the navel of the earth, the cosmic tree, and three holy mountains, all symbols of connection between sky and earth:

> And from there I went into the center of the earth and saw a blessed place, shaded with branches which live and bloom from a tree that was cut. And there I saw a holy mountain. . . . And I saw in a second direction, [another]

mountain which was higher than [the former]. . . . In the direction of the
west from this one there was [yet] another mountain, smaller than it and not
so high. (26:1-4).

So it is "from the mountain" that Yahweh speaks to Moses (19:3), not
from heaven to Moses on the mountain. Yahweh commissions Moses to
speak to the Israelites, and the speech Moses is to make begins with Yahweh's act of deliverance: Yahweh rescued them from the Egyptians and
brought them "to myself" (v. 4). Note the importance of this theological
formulation: the emphasis is not on the Israelites' escape to the desert, to
safety, or to the mountain—although all of these are true—but to God. God
is not only the deliverer, but the destination of the journey. The image of
bearing "on eagle's wings" is one of being snatched to safety by a bird
with powerful and swift wings (e.g., Deut. 28:49; Isa.40:31; Jer. 48:40;
Ezek. 17:3; Hab. 1:8).

Note that the contract which Yahweh makes with the Israelites is a con-
ditional one: their continued relationship is based upon Israel's obedience.
The reciprocity of the relationship hinges on Yahweh's initiation of deliverance and Israel's ongoing commitment. That is, while Yahweh calls for
fidelity to their relationship, the act of deliverance is first. Yahweh's act
precedes human response: grace, then gratitude. But one should also note
that this is an asymmetrical relationship, not one between equals. In the
ancient world (and in traditional societies in general), the social distance
between common folk and those who can help them is often great; a relationship between them requires an intermediary who can bridge that distance—a broker (see, e.g., Genesis 23; John 12:20-22). So in this story,
Yahweh is the patron, Israel is the client, and Moses acts as broker of the
deal. Indeed, Israel does not even receive the message directly from
Moses, but is represented by elders. Thus the social hierarchy symboled
here is: Yahweh, Moses, elders, people. And when the people affirm their
allegiance to Yahweh and the contract, this has to be reported back to Yahweh by Moses as the broker.

The result of the contract is a special patron-client relationship between
Yahweh and Israel (a treasured possession): they will be Yahweh's "priestly kingdom" and "holy people" (v. 6). Sacredness or holiness is that quality of exclusivity and being set apart for the deity. So times (feasts, fasts),
places (shrines, temples), objects (altars, the ark of the covenant), and people (priests) can all be set apart for the use of the deity. The metaphor here,
then, is that Israel as a whole has a sacral status as Yahweh's special client.
While Yahweh claims the whole earth, Israel is accorded this peculiar role
and status.

(For Hosea 5:15—6:6, see the Second Sunday after Pentecost.)

SECOND LESSON: ROMANS 5:1-11

Within the "body" of the epistle, this passage introduces a major section (5:1—8:39) that focuses on new life in Christ. It picks up the theme of "justification by faith" articulated in the previous section (1:16—4:25), and it rephrases the roles played by God, Jesus, and believers. Notice that throughout Paul uses first-person plural forms (we/us/our). God delivers the community of believers, not isolated individuals. This is a key issue in the ancient Mediterranean societies that are oriented to group relationships rather than individual experiences. This should not be underestimated by modern readers who may have learned to think of salvation in individualistic terms.

Again, it is the patron/broker/client set of relationships that Paul articulates. Peace between God (the patron) and humans (clients) is accomplished through Jesus (broker); he brokers the peace by means of his death (v. 1) and "through him we have obtained access to this grace" (v. 2). This brokerage of benefits would be a common experience for Paul's readers. The distance between those who have access to power on a daily basis are often socially too distant for common people to approach; consequently, brokers act as intermediaries to bridge that distance, and that is Paul's metaphor for Jesus' action and role.

(For Romans 4:18-25, see the Second Sunday after Pentecost.)

GOSPEL: MATTHEW 9:35—10:8(9-23)

In the narrative structure of Matthew's Gospel, this lectionary reading includes two quite distinct parts: a summary of Jesus' ministry in Galilean cities, villages, and synagogues (9:35-38), and Jesus' commissioning of the twelve disciples (10:1-42). Juxtaposed, the description of Jesus' ministry provides a fitting transition to the tasks set before the Twelve: their ministry reflects his ministry. Chapter 10 fulfills two functions: it provides the content of Jesus' commission to his inner circle; but it also speaks to the evangelist's audience as a summary of discipleship issues, answering the question, What does it mean to be called by Jesus as a disciple?

One of the clues that Matthew's urban audience is in view here (and an audience probably unacquainted with the details of Palestinian geography) is that Jesus is described as traveling, not only to villages (Gk. *komai*), but to cities (Gk. *poleis*) as well (9:35; compare "all Galilee" in Mark 1:39 and "the villages" in Mark 6:6b). But one should note that all four canonical Gospels are conspicuously silent about Jesus ever going to either of the two cities in Galilee: Sepphoris (about 3.5 miles northwest of Nazareth) and Tiberias (about 17 miles south of Capernaum on the western shore of the Sea of Galilee). Matthew also obscures the case a bit by referring to Nazareth and Bethany as "cities" (see 2:23; 21:17), when these were, in fact, quite small villages. As far as we can determine from our sources, the earliest Jesus movement was restricted to Galilean villages and towns.

A clue to Matthew's polemical concerns is that he refers to Jesus preaching in "their synagogues" (9:35). This seems to reflect the end of the first century when a clear demarcation had developed between the followers of Jesus, who had severed ties with local synagogues, and the rest of the Judeans around the Mediterranean. The lines of in-group and out-group had developed further in the last quarter of the first century, with the "scribes and Pharisees" representing the epitome of Judeans hostile to the Jesus movement (see, e.g., Matt. 5:20; 12:38-42; 15:1-20; 16:5-12; 23:1-36).

As a summary of what Jesus' ministry is about, vv. 35-36 serve well; indeed, Matthew has already used the words of v. 35 in 4:23 as the lead into the "Sermon on the Mount." First, he proclaims "the good news of the kingdom." This is a summary phrase, similar to those found throughout the Synoptic Gospels, which identifies his message as one of deliverance, joy, and hope. It also incorporates an abbreviated form of his program "God's reign." The English word *reign* seems to capture the sense of the Greek *basileus* here, since it refers to God's status as supreme patron and God's benevolent kingship, rather than kingdom, which can easily be misconstrued as a location. Second, Jesus heals every illness and infirmity. "Healing" (RSV; Gk. *therapeuō*) is a more appropriate translation than "curing" (NRSV), since the former conveys the model of illness-intervention by a healer in a traditional society better than the latter, which conveys a modern medical model of bacteriology and virology. In modern parlance, "illness" also fits the traditional model better than "disease" (RSV and NRSV) for the same reason (see John J. Pilch, "Sickness and Healing in Luke-Acts," in *The Social World of Luke-Acts*, ed. J. H. Neyrey [Peabody, Mass.: Hendrickson, 1991], 181–209). Third, Jesus' compassion for the crowds who are "harassed and helpless" speaks to the social conditions of first-century Galilean peasants, and Jesus' response with care, emotion, and relationship. During Jesus' ministry, Galilee was ruled by Herod Antipas (a Roman client and a son of Herod the Great). The people were subject to taxes, tolls, tribute, and tithes imposed by the Roman emperor, the Herodian "tetrarch," and the Jerusalem temple and priests. These were people who were in need of some good news.

The "plentiful harvest" saying (vv. 37-38) is an independent aphorism which stands alone in *Gos. Thom.* 73, and opens Jesus' commissioning of the Seventy in Luke 10:2. It may also be reflected in John 4:35. To what the metaphor of harvest refers in this saying is not self-evident. It is certainly taken by the canonical evangelists as a metaphor relating to spreading the good news, since it is set in the literary context of the commissioning of the Twelve (Matthew), the commissioning of the Seventy (Luke), and Jesus' success in Samaria (John). But what type of gathering at harvest this implies is a bit fuzzy, especially since further along in the Gospel Matthew uses the metaphor of harvest as "the close of the age" (13:39). Perhaps it refers to bringing the proclamation of God's reign and fatherhood to fruition in the form of community. Another way of stating this might be to think of the harvest as the climactic process in which the harassment and helplessness (9:36) comes to a head and is given definition in God's reign.

Matthew 10:1-8 is composed of three parts: a narrative summary of the disciples' commission (v. 1), a listing of the disciples' names (vv. 2-5), and the first part of Jesus' commissioning speech (vv. 6-8); the whole commissioning speech is 10:6-42. The narrative summary in 10:1 describes the mission of the Twelve as including exorcism and healing. These two actions point back to the two preceding passages: in 9:32-34 Jesus exorcises a demon, and in 9:35 the same phrase is used of Jesus "healing every illness and infirmity" (see also 15:29-31). This mission of healing for Jesus and the Twelve make it clear that God's reign is expressed in the care of whole persons, not "saving souls."

The names of the Twelve seem to be listed in three groups of four:

Simon, called Peter	Philip	James, Alphaeus' son
Andrew, his brother	Bartholemew	Thaddaeus
James, Zebedee's son	Thomas	Simon, the Canaanean
John, his brother	Matthew, the toll-collector	Judas Iscariot, who betrayed him

Several things stand out in how the list is presented. First, Simon is not only listed first, he is also identified as first. Second, Judas is not only listed last, but he is identified already as the betrayer before the reader gets to the passion narrative. Third, the identifying labels for their names are of five types: an alternative name (Simon/Peter), kinship association (Andrew, James, John, James), possibly hometown (Simon of Cana?), profession (Matthew), and the only hostile label—"who betrayed him" (Judas). And fourth, Philip, Bartholemew, Thomas, and Thaddaeus stand out as having no identifying labels at all. (For the name shift from Levi to Matthew, see the Second Sunday after Pentecost, Matt. 9:9-13, 18-26.)

Jesus' commissioning speech begins with a negative: They should not go to Gentiles (non-Judeans) or Samaritans (lest there be any confusion over the definition of Samaritans as belonging to "the house of Israel" or not). The phrase "lost sheep of the house of Israel" picks up the theme from Jesus' compassion over the people in 9:36; but Matthew is the only Gospel to indicate a limitation to "Israelites" for the Jesus mission (contrast Mark 6:7-13; Luke 9:1-6). The rest of the imperatives are preach, heal, raise, cleanse, exorcise. The mission of the Twelve was to spread Jesus' message of God's reign, as well as to be agents of restoration to whole persons, addressing illness, death, impurity, and demon-possession.

(For Matthew 9:9-13, see the Second Sunday after Pentecost.)

HOMILETICAL CONSIDERATIONS

Jesus' commissioning of the Twelve speaks to how the gospel addresses fundamental human need at every level: sickness, death, impurity, and evil. But the commission also speaks to God's deliverance as gift in the terse formulation: "You received without payment; give without payment" (or: "You received [as] gift; give [as] gift"). The church is so easily defined as institution, corporation, or simply as a group of high ethical standards. But at the heart of the church's identity is the call to be the conduit of God's gracious gifts. As that grace envelops, surrounds, and overwhelms us, our brokenness is healed, our death is turned to life, our pollution is purified, our evil is cast out. But this healing is not for ourselves alone; it then begins to pervade all our relationships. But the giving does not decrease our gifts, it increases them. There is no gospel but the "social gospel," because the gospel is about receiving and giving, about being healed and reaching out to heal others.

Fourth Sunday after Pentecost
Eleventh Sunday in Ordinary Time
Proper 7

Lectionary	First Lesson	Psalm	Second Lesson	Gospel
Revised Common	Jer. 20:7-13	Ps. 69:7-10 (11-15), 16-18	Rom. 6:1b-11	Matt. 10:24-39
Episcopal (BCP)	Jer. 20:7-13	Ps. 69:1-18 *or* 69:7-10, 16-18	Rom. 5:15b-19	Matt. 10: (16-23) 24-33
Roman Catholic	Exod. 19:2-6	Ps. 100:1-3, 5	Rom. 5:6-11	Matt. 9:36—10:8
Lutheran (LBW)	Exod. 19:2-8a	Psalm 100	Rom. 5:6-11	Matt. 9:35—10:8

FIRST LESSON: JEREMIAH 20:7-13

This poetry is simultaneously elegant and heart-wrenching as the prophet expresses pain and torment followed by confidence and praise. The depth of emotion and richness of metaphor in this passage is extremely powerful. It is a fitting scenario for the life of faith lived out in the tension between despair and hope, sorrow and joy. But it has special power in this literary context, articulating the prophet's role as spokesperson for God, and therefore bearing the brunt of negative public response to calls for justice and righteousness.

The poem is cast in the classic form of a complaint song, a form often mislabeled by commentators as "lament." True laments (e.g., 2 Sam. 1:19-27; Lamentations 1; 2) pour out grief concerning situations that cannot be substantively changed (e.g., a dead king, a destroyed city), and they are absent from the Psalter. But complaints are common among the Psalms, and they call upon God to intervene and act on behalf of the petitioner. I note as parallels here formal elements from several classical individual complaint songs: Psalms 3, 5, 6, 7, 17, and 22. The introduction is an *invocation*, the calling upon Yahweh by name (v. 7; see, e.g., Pss. 3:1; 5:1; 6:1; 17:1). The invocation not only identifies the object of petition, but is personal and relational; that Yahweh reveals his names to Moses creates entrée for Israel (see Exod. 3:13-15; 6:2-4). The *complaint proper* is the next traditional element; using indicative verbs, it identifies and describes the problem/s that elicit/s the crying out to God: usually persecution by enemies, illness, or a sense of God's abandonment (see, e.g., Pss. 12:1-2; 13:1-2; 17:10-12; 22:1-2). The prophet's complaint in vv. 7-10 comes down to two issues: he is under the compulsion of the divine word, despite his strong desire to avoid it (vv. 7a-b, 8-9); and the result of this divine compulsion is that the community humiliates him, shames him, and plots against him (vv. 7c-d, 10). The prophet, therefore, is caught in the double bind of divine power (and expectations) and public shame (and rejection), the two most potent forces in traditional societies. The struggle is not to discern what is right—that is clear. The poet is grappling with the painful, indeed dangerous, consequences of responding to and dealing with God.

These frightening images break, however, with the transition of "but" in v. 11. This begins the next stage in the complaint song: the *affirmation of trust*. This expresses hope in Yahweh's goodness and power to act on the supplicant's behalf (see, e.g., Pss. 3:3-6; 5:4-6; 7:10-11; 12:7; 13:5; 22:3-5, 27-31). The poet/prophet's trust lies in Yahweh's presence ("Yahweh is with me") and power ("like a dread warrior"; "Yahweh of the armies"), recalling the images of Yahweh expressed in the so-called "Song of Miriam" (Exod. 15:21) and its expansion in the "Song of the Sea" (Exod. 15:1-18): "Yahweh is a warrior, Yahweh is his name" (Exod. 15:3); "Sing to Yahweh, for he has triumphed gloriously; horse and rider he has cast into the sea" (15:21). Because it is Yahweh's word that the prophet proclaims, it is to Yahweh that the prophet commits his cause (v. 12d). He trusts that Yahweh will turn the tables on his enemies: they will stumble and not prevail (v. 11b-c), they will be shamed and dishonored in perpetuity (v. 11d-e).

The conclusion is the *hymn*, praising Yahweh's person and work (Pss. 3:8; 5:11-12; 7:17; 13:6). The prophet proclaims Yahweh's power to deliver the "needy" (the socially desperate) from evildoers (v. 13). Thus the movement of the song is linear: from desperation to vindication. And the prophet's hope is founded in God's character; the prophet's own power cannot turn things around, only God's. But the audience (ancient or modern) should not be misled by the linear movement; this is not a "quick fix" solution to the poet's situation. The affirmation of trust and hymn articulate hope rooted in relationship. They take the long view, and recognize that vindication entails process, not event. The tension of the poet's pain is not simply brushed aside, but deeply felt and expressed. Giving voice to the pain creates relationship between the petitioner and the petitioned. The hope resides in that relational dynamic.

(For Exodus 19:2-8a, see the Third Sunday after Pentecost.)

PSALM 69

Like the prophet's song in Jer. 20:7-13, this psalm is a complaint song of the individual; and it includes most of the traditional elements discussed above: an invocation and cry (v. 1a), complaint proper (vv. 1b-12), supplication (vv. 13-18), complaint proper (vv. 19-21), supplication (vv. 22-29), a vow of praise (vv. 30-33), and, finally, a hymn (vv. 34-36). The new elements here are fully developed *supplications* or *petitions*. These employ imperative verbs, calling upon God to act in specific ways: answer (v. 13b), rescue (v. 14a), deliver (v. 14b), do not let . . . sweep, swallow up, or close (v. 15), answer (v. 16a), turn toward (v. 16b), do not hide (v. 17a), draw near (v. 18a), redeem (18a), set free (v. 18b), let . . . be a trap (v. 22a), let . . . be darkened (v. 23a), make tremble (v. 23b), pour out (v. 24a), let . . . overtake (v. 24b). The number and diversity of these petitions articulate the depth of emotion and desperation.

Like the song in Jeremiah, the psalmist complains of harassment, public humiliation, and attack by enemies (vv. 4a-d, 9-12, 19-20, 26). The additional problems identified are: false accusations of theft (v. 4e), exile (v. 8), and poisoning (v. 21). As a further parallel to the Jeremiah poem, the psalmist claims that the reason for harassment is commitment to Yahweh (vv. 9-11). One of the recurring metaphors of the psalmist's precarious state is water. While rain and springs are positive images in Israelite literature, the sea and the deep are metaphors of chaos and danger. These waters are unpredictable, uncontrollable, and frightening. Thus, the poet expresses a sense of peril in relation to the waters (v. 1b), deep mire (v. 2a), deep waters (v. 2b), the flood (v. 2c), the mire (v. 14a), deep waters (v. 14c), the flood (v. 15a), the deep (v. 15b). The creative forces of order are embattled by the forces of a watery chaos. In most Israelite literature the mythological elements of this chaos are limited to poetic metaphor; but it occasionally takes grander shape, such as in Yahweh's swordfight with the chaos monsters, Rahab and Leviathan (Isa. 51:9-11).

Psalms such as this likely derive from real situations of crisis in Israelite/Judahite life. But it is helpful to remember that their longevity of use in the Psalter as the community's "hymnbook" derives from the openness to more general applications: they express the emotions and experience of more than one person in a unique situation.

SECOND LESSON: ROMANS 5:15B-19; 6:1B-11

Romans 5:15b-19. In Rom. 5:12-21 Paul contrasts Adam and Christ in addressing the universal human experience of death. This fits in with the section on "new life in Christ" (5:1—8:39). The apostle used this mythic contrast of Adam and Christ in 1 Corinthians to argue for the reality and significance of Christ's resurrection (1 Cor. 15:20-28, 42-50). It is "mythic" in the sense of *foundational*, a story or symbol-set to which one appeals for a fundamental understanding of some aspect of the community's identity. It is not simply any story—or even history—but *a story that defines and interprets reality* for the intended audience. Adam's relevance does not stem from the ability to verify that he was a historical character; it stems from his symbolic status as primal ancestor and character in the first biblical story of sin. Both Adam and Christ are cosmic in their significance. The binary oppositions Paul uses are:

Adam	Jesus
sin	righteousness/justification
trespass	grace
disobedience	obedience
condemnation	acquittal
death	life

Adam plays virtually no role in the Israelite tradition apart from Gen. 2:4b—3:24. But in the hellenistic period, both Judean and Christian literatures gave him more attention (for references, see J. H. Charlesworth, ed., *The Old Testament Pseudepigrapha*, 2 vols. [Garden City, N.Y.: Doubleday, 1983]; the dates given are very rough approximations). The Genesis stories of Adam and Eve's creation and sin is retold in: *Jubilees* (second cent. B.C.E.), where Adam is also described, not only as the first man (chaps. 2–4), but the first person to be buried in the earth (4:29-30); the *Apocalypse of Abraham* (first cent. C.E.), where they are tempted by the demon Azazel (chap. 23); and the *Life of Adam and Eve* (first cent. C.E.), where the pair repent. In *2 Enoch* (first cent. C.E.), it is predicted that Adam will be escorted in the last days into the third heaven (chap. 42, longer version). In the *Apocalypse of Adam* (first to fourth cent. C.E.), Adam passes on his esoteric vision and knowledge to his son Seth. And in the *Testament of Adam* (Christian, second to fifth cent. C.E.), Adam explains the secrets of creation to Seth; predicts the birth, death, and resurrection of Christ; and foretells the end of world. All of this is to say that during the period from the second cent. B.C.E. to the fifth cent. C.E. Adam became an important symbol in the literatures of both Judeans and followers of Jesus as primal human, archetypal sinner, and one privy to the secrets of the universe.

But the closest parallels to Paul's point here in Romans is found in 2 Esdras, in the Old Testament Apocrypha. This is a composite work, comprising a Judean apocalypse (chaps. 3–14; also known as 4 Ezra; written c. 90 C.E.), and two Christian appendices: chaps. 1–2 (5 Ezra; second cent. C.E.) and chaps. 15–16 (6 Ezra; third cent. C.E.). The key passages are:

> For the first Adam, burdened with an evil heart, transgressed and was overcome, as were also all who were descended from him. Thus the disease became permanent; the law was in the hearts of the people along with the evil root; but what was good departed, and the evil remained. (3:21-22; see also 4:30)

> For an evil heart has grown up in us, which has alienated us from God, and

> has brought us into corruption and the ways of death, and has shown us the paths of perdition and removed us far from life—and that not merely for a few but for almost all who have been created. (7:48)

Paul certainly differs from 2 Esdras 7:48, in that he would not agree with "almost all" being far from life. For Paul, it is most definitely all, because the logic of his argument is that all have equal need of God's grace because all have sinned (see, e.g., Rom. 3:23; 5:12, 18; 11:32; Gal. 3:22). Just as no one is exempt from culpability, no one is beyond the reach of God's grace. Later in 2 Esdras, one finds agreement with Paul's line of argument on both counts:

> For in truth there is no one among those who have been born who has not acted wickedly; among those who have existed there is no one who has not done wrong. For in this, O Lord, your righteousness and goodness will be declared, when you are merciful to those who have no store of good works. (8:35-36)

The important difference for Paul is that this mercy of God is effected through Christ's death (see also 1 Thess. 5:9-10); the cross is decisive. For a somewhat different set of metaphors contrasting the former situation of death with the present situation of life, see 2 Cor. 3:7-11.

Romans 6:1b-11. "Heaven forbid!" (KJV), "By no means!" (RSV, NRSV), "Hell no!" (Cotton Patch Version). These are some of the translations for Paul's *mê genoito* in response to rhetorical questions that he identifies as representing absolutely offensive or ridiculous conclusions. He uses this phrase ten times in Romans (and elsewhere only in Gal. 2:17 and 3:21):

> "Does their faithlessness nullify their faith in God?" (3:3-4)
> ". . . what shall we say? That God is unjust to inflict wrath on us?" (3:5-6)
> "Do we then overthrow the law by this faith?" (3:31)
> "What shall we say then? Are we to continue in sin that grace may
>   abound?" (6:2)
> "What then? Are we to sin because we are not under law but under
>   grace?" (6:15)
> "What then shall we say? That the law is sin?" (7:7)
> "Did that which is good, then, bring death to me?" (7:13)
> "What shall we say then? That there is injustice on God's part?" (9:14)
> "I ask, then, has God rejected his people?" (11:1)
> "I ask, then, have they stumbled so as to fall?" (11:11)

Paul poses these questions in order to refute them: God's justice, the status of the law, the relationship of grace and faith, and the status of Israel. But more than refutation: He wants to make absolutely sure that the reader does not confuse these with his own positions. On the one hand, this is an effective rhetorical device. On the other, the vehemence with which he cuts these positions off may stem from: (*a*) having had to defend himself against accusations that these are indeed natural conclusions based on his theology (see, e.g., Rom. 3:8); or (*b*) having had to refute such theological positions held by his opponents (see, e.g., 1 Cor. 6:12-20).

That some of Paul's opponents may have held "libertine" positions, as addressed here in Romans 6, is possible (see 1 Cor. 5:1-2); but it may just be a hypothetical construct for heightened rhetorical effect. As Paul represents it, his opponents' syllogism here would then be:

If (*a*) our sin prompts God's grace;
and (*b*) the more grace we receive, the better off we are;
then (*c*) we should continue sinning to increase the flow of God's grace.

Besides his adamant "NO!" Paul's argument is based upon what happens in baptism: one participates fully in Christ's death and resurrection. This being the case, the old life of sin is left behind: why would someone who has "died to sin" want to continue to wallow in it? His formulation to the Galatians parallels this: "As many as you as were baptized into Christ have put on Christ" (Gal. 3:27).

(For Romans 5:6-11, see the Third Sunday after Pentecost.)

GOSPEL: MATTHEW 10:(16-23)24-39

Chapter 10 as a whole is a discourse on discipleship, the second of five major discourses in the Gospel: the message of God's reign (chaps. 5–7); discipleship (10); parables (13); in-group discipline (18); and judgment (24–25). It begins with "Then Jesus summoned his twelve disciples . . ." (10:1), and, parallel to the other discourses, it concludes with a completion formula: "Now when Jesus had finished instructing his twelve disciples . . ." (11:1; see 7:28; 13:53; 19:1; 26:1). By collecting sayings around individual topics, the evangelist has constructed five "books" parallel to the five books of Moses (Genesis to Deuteronomy). (For the first part of Matthew 10, see the Third Sunday after Pentecost; for the two concluding passages in the chapter [vv. 34-39 and 40-42], see the Fifth Sunday after Pentecost.)

Most of this material in Matthew 10 is the evangelist's adaptation of sayings from the Gospel's two main literary sources: Mark and Q (the hypothetical "Sayings Source" used by both Matthew and Luke). Matthew 10:17-22 is adapted from Mark 13, and 10:26-33 is Q material paralleled in Luke 12. But additional parallels to the individual aphorisms—in John, *Gospel of Thomas*, *2 Clement* (c. 150 C.E.), and the Oxyrhynchus Papyri (fragmentary Greek manuscripts discovered in Egypt)—demonstrate that this section is comprised of numerous individual sayings gathered into a single "speech" Jesus along thematic lines:

Sheep among wolves	Matt. 10:16a	// Luke 10:3; *2 Clem.* 5:2-4
Serpents & doves	Matt. 10:16b	// *Gos. Thom.* 39; POxy. 655:2; Rom. 16:19
Delivered up to authorities	Matt. 10:17-18	// Matt.24:9; Mark 13:9; Luke 21:12
Spirit will provide words	Matt. 10:19-20	// Mark 13:11; Luke 12:11; 21:15; John 14:26
Delivered up by family	Matt. 10:21	// Mic 7:6; Mark 13:12
Hated for Jesus' sake	Matt. 10:22a	// Mark 13:13a; John 15:18
Endure to the end	Matt. 10:22b	// Matt. 24:13; Mark 13:13b; Luke 21:19
Persecuted town to town	Matt.10:23	// Matt. 23:34
Disciple/teacher; owner/slave	Matt. 10:24-25a	// Mark 9:35; 10:43b-45; Luke 9:48b; 22:26b-27; John 13:16; 15:20a
Beelzebul accusation	Matt. 10:25b	// Matt. 9:34; 12:24; Mark 3:22; Luke 11:15
Covered & revealed	Matt. 10:26	// Mark 4:22; Luke 8:17; 12:2; *Gos. Thom.* 5-6; POxy. 654:5
Proclaim on the rooftops	Matt. 10:27	// Luke 12:3; *Gos. Thom.* 33; POxy. 1:8
Killing body and soul	Matt. 10:28	// Luke 12:4-5
A sparrow's fall	Matt. 10:29-31	// Luke 12:6-7; [21:18]
Acknowledgment & denial	Matt. 10:32-33	// Luke 12:8-9; *2 Clem.* 3:2

The theme that runs throughout the whole passage might be formulated as "faithful perseverance in the face of persecution." Even the sayings that do not directly relate to this theme are subsumed under them. For example, the sayings about revealing the covered (v. 26) and proclaiming from the rooftops (v. 27) are general aphorisms about revelation and proclamation; but here they are introduced with the phrase "So have no fear of them," putting them in the context of relating to persecutors.

What emerges from this long string of aphorisms is: (*a*) persecution is an expected part of discipleship, given the treatment of Jesus (vv. 17-18, 21-22a, 23-25; (*b*) do not be afraid, because God cares and is with you in your pain and trouble (vv. 19-20, 26-31); and (*c*) perseverance and acknowledgment of Jesus leads to deliverance and acknowledgment before the Father (vv. 22b, 32-33). The highly adaptable aphorism comparing disciple to teacher and owner to slave (vv. 24-25a) is used here as the key to understanding persecution: the life of discipleship is life in the path carved out by Jesus, including his sufferings (see, e.g., Rom. 8:17; 2 Cor. 1:5-7; Phil. 1:27-30; 3:10; 1 Thess. 2:14-15).

(For Matt. 9:35—10:8, see the Fourth Sunday after Pentecost.)

Fifth Sunday after Pentecost
Twelfth Sunday in Ordinary Time
Proper 8

Lectionary	First Lesson	Psalm	Second Lesson	Gospel
Revised Common	Jer. 28:5-9	Ps. 89:1-4, 15-18	Rom. 6:12-23	Matt. 10:40-42
Episcopal (BCP)	Isa. 2:10-17	Ps. 89:1-18 *or* 89:1-4, 15-18	Rom. 6:3-11	Matt. 10: 34-42
Roman Catholic	Jer. 20:10-13	Ps. 69:8-10, 14, 17, 33-35	Rom. 5:12-15	Matt. 10:26-33
Lutheran (LBW)	Jer. 20:7-13	Ps. 69:1-20	Rom. 5:12-15	Matt. 10:24-33

FIRST LESSON: ISAIAH 2:10-17; JEREMIAH 28:5-9

Isaiah 2:10-17. The complete poetic unit includes 2:5-22, and is cast as a prophetic threat speech. The speech begins with an *appeal* ("Come, let us walk in Yahweh's light," v. 5), followed by an *accusation* against "the house of Jacob" ("For you have forsaken," v. 6), and a *description* of the foreign idolaters to whom Jacob is attracted ("Their land is filled with idols," vv. 6b-9). In vv. 10-21, which includes the lectionary passage, the prophet makes a series of *threats* against Jacob (presumably the northern kingdom of Israel in the literary context of the book), articulating the destruction that comes to those who honor anything or anyone above Yahweh. The conclusion (v. 22) circles back to another *appeal* to "turn away from mortals." Ending with a *rhetorical question* as part of the appeal ("for of what account are they?") has a powerful effect. First, the answer should be obvious to the audience, given the preceding argument. And second, it puts the ball in the audience's court: a genuine response is called for.

The interrelated focal issues in this poem are Jacob's allegiance and Yahweh's incomparable honor. If Jacob has divided loyalties, if his relationship to Yahweh is unclear, then now is the time to change directions ("walk," v. 5; "turn," v. 22). Furthermore, this divided loyalty and infidelity constitutes a hostile challenge to Yahweh's honor. This recalls two of the fundamental tenets of Israel's identity encoded in the Decalog: no other gods before (or besides) Yahweh (Exod. 20:3), and no graven images (Exod. 20:4-6). That is, Yahweh has a unique relationship with Israel, and the worship of Yahweh precludes the use of pictures or statues of deity, presumably of either Yahweh or other gods.

The poetic repetitions highlight the focus on honor and shame. In vv. 11 and 17 the contrast is drawn between human arrogance and pride set over against Yahweh's exaltation (see also v. 9). This will take place "on that day," a recurring motif in the prophetic literature for the day of Yahweh's reckoning accounts (see, e.g., Isa. 3:7; Jer. 4:9; Hos. 1:5; Joel 1:15; Amos 2:16; Mic. 2:4). The second set of repetitions is in vv. 10 and 19: these boastful, high, haughty idol worshipers will be running for cover in the rocks and dust, the caves and holes, when confronted with Yahweh's terror (Heb. *pachad*). This frightening image hearkens back to one of the ancient epithets in the "patriarchal sagas," where God is called "the Fear/Terror of Isaac" (*pachad yitzchaq*; Gen. 31:42, 53). And what these arrogant ones will find so terrifying is "the glory of his majesty," that is, Yahweh's royal honor.

Two things about this passage lead to the conclusion that this text may in fact derive from Deutero-Isaiah (Isaiah 40–55; c. 550–540 B.C.E.) during the Babylonian exile (598–539 B.C.E.), rather than Isaiah of Jerusalem (Isaiah 1–35; c. 740–700 B.C.E.). The first is that Deutero-Isaiah repeatedly addresses the issue of the worthlessness of "idol worship" (Isa. 41:21-29; 44:9-20; and 45:20-25; see the Eighth Sunday after Pentecost, Isa. 44:6-8 and Wis. 12:13, 16-19). And the second is that "the house of Jacob" is an epithet which Deutero-Isaiah adapts for Judah in exile (Isa. 46:3; 48:1) from the older Isaiah material, where it seems to refer to the northern kingdom of Israel (e.g., Isa. 8:17; 10:20; 29:22). Whatever chronological era one identifies for this poem, it should be interpreted in light of the whole book's interest in loyalty to Yahweh as the patron-god of both Israel and Judah, and the polemic against idol worship. That this polemic was necessary for more than one era can be seen even for followers of Jesus at the end of the first century C.E. (1 John 5:21)!

Jeremiah 28 narrates the encounters between two prophets, Jeremiah and Hananiah, but the passage needs to be seen in the context of Jeremiah 27–29. The time frame provided by the editor is "the beginning of the reign of Zedekiah, the Judahite king, in the fifth month of the fourth year" (28:1), which in our calendar would be August of 594 B.C.E. The fourth year refers to the fourth year of the Babylonian exile of many Judahites (598 B.C.E.; see 2 Kgs. 24:1-16). Zedekiah (formerly named Mattaniah) was the uncle of Jehoiachin, the exiled Judahite king (2 Kgs. 24:17-20). And the location for both Hananiah's prophecy and Jeremiah's reply is the temple, in the presence of both priests and the general population (28:1, 5).

Hananiah's name (*Chananyahu*) means "Yahweh is gracious" ("Yahu" being one of the short forms of the divine name "Yahweh"); but the meaning of Jeremiah's name (*Yirmeyahu*) depends upon which Hebrew verb forms the first part of the name: *rûm* or *ramah*. If it is the first, then his name means "Yahweh is exalted"; if it is the second, it could mean: (*a*) "Yahweh is treacherous/deceitful"; (*b*) "Yahweh loosens" (presumably, loosens the womb); or (*c*) "Yahweh shoots" (a bow).

Hananiah's name is most significant here because he forthrightly proclaims Yahweh's gracious deliverance of the Judahite exiles from Babylon, with Yahweh breaking "the yoke of Babylon's king" (28:4). This is in response to Jeremiah wearing a yoke and thongs on his neck at Yahweh's order (27:2), and prophesying that Babylon's hegemony over the Near East was at Yahweh's instigation. This prophecy was directed to Judah's neighbors, evidently involved with Judah in an anti-Babylonian conspiracy (27:3-11); Zedekiah, the Judahite king (27:12-15); and the Judahite priests and general population (27:16-22). Prophets proclaiming a quick peace are specifically identified in 27:9-10 and 16-18 and are dismissed as liars. So when Hananiah speaks in 28:1-4, the reader immediately is clued into the interpretative context for such a prophecy (see also Deut. 18:15-22; Jer. 6:13-14; 23:16-22; 29:8-9).

All of this, then, sets the stage for Jeremiah's response in the lectionary reading (28:5-9). It is not a prophecy, but a warning based upon tradition. He first indicates that he surely desires what Hananiah has prophesied: peace and restoration (v. 6). But this is followed in v. 7 by a "yet" (read: Hold on, Hananiah!). The problem, Jeremiah warns, is that Hananiah's prophecy of peace flies in the face of the Israelite and Judahite prophetic tradition: their primary task as prophets "from ancient times" was to warn, threaten, or announce "war, famine, and pestilence" (v. 8); so a prophecy of disaster would be entirely expected. Jeremiah warns Hananiah that prophesying peace is a trickier affair; whether it was appropriate or not would take time (v. 9). Hananiah responds by breaking Jeremiah's wooden yoke and reiterating his prophecy of deliverance (vv. 10-11). But then the Yahweh word comes to Jeremiah that Hananiah was a liar who would be punished with death (vv. 12-16): "In that same year, in the seventh month, the prophet Hananiah died" (v. 17). Clearly, a critical element in the appropriateness of a prophecy is timing.

The function of this account is to provide a paradigmatic case for the audience of lying prophets (see Jer. 29:8-9). It also depicts Judah's internal struggles over public policy in the face of disastrous circumstances. And chapter 28 provides two responses to Hananiah's prophecy of peace: it runs counter to tradition, and Yahweh has identified it as a lie. But latent in the text is also a sense of ambiguity in prophecies: even Jeremiah, the true prophet, could not tell the difference between the Yahweh word he had received and Hananiah's supposed Yahweh word! While he was wary, he still allowed Hananiah to take the yoke from his neck (28:10-11). The falsity of the prophecy did not rest in its content, but its timing and its origin: in wish fulfillment rather than God.

(For Jeremiah 20:7-13, see the Fourth Sunday after Pentecost.)

SECOND LESSON: ROMANS 5:12-15; 6:12-23

For the importance of Adam in Romans and the use of "By no means!" see above on the Fourth Sunday after Pentecost (Rom. 5:15b-19 and 6:1b-11). In Rom. 5:12-21 Paul poses Adam and Christ as binary opposites. And this reading fits in with the larger section on "New Life in Christ" (5:1—8:39). **Romans 5:12-15.** Significant here is Paul's formulation of the "one" and "all" or "the many." In vv. 12-14, Paul describes the deficit position of humanity: sin entered the world through "one human" (Gk. *henos anthrôpou*), sin brought death, and death became the reality for "all humans" (*pantes anthropous*). This he contrasts in v. 15 with the new situation: God's grace through "the one human" (Gk. *tou henos anthrôpou*), Jesus Christ, is effective for "the many" (*tous pollous*). In English, we would read "the many" as restrictive: numerous, but not quite all. But this is a Greek idiomatic expression for "all," as can be seen in the beginning of the verse: "For if many (*hoi polloi*) died. . . ." Clearly, all humans have died. Just as sin and death are not limited to one group (or only the most heinous deviants), so God's grace is not limited to one group (or only the most deserving). If Adam is the archetypal human as the embodiment of death, then Jesus is also an archetypal human: the embodiment of God's grace (*charis*). This type of formulation would resonate well with Mediterranean social structures, which perceived all individuals as embedded in someone else or some larger group. Furthermore, this grace cannot possibly be received as payment for performance, but only as gift (*dôrea*). Despite the variety of ways Paul has been interpreted throughout the centuries, this point could hardly be overlooked or made subservient to other issues given the number of times Paul returns to it (see, e.g., Rom. 3:24; 6:23; 11:29; 1 Cor. 4:7; 2 Cor. 9:15). **Romans 6:12-23.** Continuing his argument about sin, death, the law, and grace, Paul highlights here the ethical dimension of the discussion: "to obey" (Gk. *hupakouô*; vv. 12, 16, 17). The two sets of metaphors he employs here are slavery and purity. Beginning with the presupposition that everyone is "slave" to something (v. 16), he argues that we have been released from one form of slavery, which is binding, limiting, and degenerative: "slaves of sin" (*douloi tês hamartias*; vv. 17, 20). The new status is to become "enslaved to righteousness" (vv. 18) or "enslaved of God" (v. 22), which is life-giving. For Paul's audiences, slavery was a potent symbol, for it was pervasive in the Roman Empire of the first century; indeed, Rome was the first true "slave society"—a society whose economy and social structure was heavily dependent upon slave labor. And, indeed, the metaphor of "slavery to sin" was evidently common enough among early Jesus groups and Judeans: "Truly, truly, I say to you: everyone who commits sin is a slave to sin" (*doulos tês hamartias*; John 8:34); "They promise them freedom, but are themselves slaves of corruption (*douloi tês phthoras*); for whatever overcomes a person, to that he is enslaved (*dedoulôtai*)" (2 Pet. 2:19); "wisdom will not enter a deceitful soul, nor dwell in a body enslaved to sin (*katachreô hamartias*)" (Wis. 1:4); "For if they had been enslaved to emotions (*tois pathesin doulôthentes*) . . . we would say that they had been conquered by these emotions" (4 Macc. 13:2; see also 3:2).

The second metaphor Paul introduces is "purity." The former situation Paul describes as physically yielding to impurity (*akatharsia*) and increasing iniquity (or lawlessness, *anomia*; v. 19b), which ends in death (v. 21):

impurity → increased lawlessness → death

Because of the new life in Christ, Paul challenges the audience to now yield to "righteousness" (*dikaiosûnê*) for "sanctification" (*haiasmon*) (v. 19c). He goes on to say that sanctification leads to "eternal life" (*zôên aiônion*; v. 22):

righteousness → sanctification → eternal life

He has no specific ethical injunctions or warnings to make here; this is a programmatic statement that there are ethical consequences to being freed, purified, and joined with Christ.

(For Romans 6:3-11, see the Fourth Sunday after Pentecost.)

GOSPEL: MATTHEW 10:34-42

The two passages included in this lectionary reading (vv. 34-39 and 40-42) form the conclusion of the discourse on discipleship, the second of five major discourses in the Gospel. (For the earlier parts of Matthew 10, see the Third and Fourth Sundays after Pentecost.)

The first section (vv. 34-39) addresses the stark realities and uncompromising expectations of attachment to Jesus. The reality was that joining a Jesus group in the late first century could mean family discord, the breaking apart of the fundamental social structure. In fact, this section includes five independent sayings woven together:

Not peace, but a sword	Matt. 10:34	// Luke 12:51; *Gos. Thom.* 16a
Alienation of families	Matt. 10:35-36	// Mic. 7:6; Matt. 10:21; Mark 13:12;Luke 12:52-53; *Gos. Thom.* 16b)
Comparative love	Matt. 10:37	// Luke 14:26; *Gos. Thom.* 55a, 101)

| Taking up the cross | Matt. 10:38 | // Matt. 16:24; Mark 8:34; Luke 9:23; 14:27; *Gos. Thom.* 55b) |
| Finding and losing life | Matt. 10:39 | // Matt. 16:25; Mark 8:35; Luke 9:24; 17:33; John 12:25) |

These are linked together differently (or kept separate) in different Gospels, so that it becomes clear that Matthew has shaped a unique complex on the consequences of associating with Jesus and his faction (but note that the first and second were already combined by Q, as the fourth and fifth were in Mark). What unites them is the common, startling theme of discipleship and death: the "sword" (v. 34), an alienated "household" (vv. 35-36), love greater than family (v. 37), the "cross" (v. 38), and "losing life" (v. 39). These metaphors operate at two levels: physical death and social death. The cross was no pallid metaphor to Mediterranean people who had seen both Roman and Judean (Hasmonean and Herodian) rulers crucify murderers, revolutionaries, and social bandits for being a threat to the state. But obviously not everyone who became a disciple of Jesus was killed.

Besides physical death, however, was the threat of social death: exile and alienation from one's kin group, village, guild, synagogue (indeed, these configurations were overlapping and interlocking). The bottomline is that Jesus' call to discipleship was a call to risk, to venture, to leap. The flipside is that the risk is worth it; the conclusion is "those who lose their life for my sake will find it!" (v. 39). To leave one's family of origin and follow Jesus was to become part of Jesus' fictive family. It is the fictive kin group that Jesus is gathering which is so socially scandalous: toll collectors, unattached women, and prostitutes! Just as Jesus redefines "family," he redefines "life."

(For Matthew 10:24-33, see the Fourth Sunday after Pentecost.)

HOMILETICAL CONSIDERATIONS

Paul Tillich articulated that much of what plagues our daily lives is anxiety, which remains unfocused and unnamed. But the terror that underlies our ordinary fears is death (*The Courage to Be* [New Haven: Yale University Press, 1952]). We fear the power of others over us could lead to death; we fear that our incompetent actions could lead to death; we fear that faceless institutions could demolish us. What happens in Matthew's collection of Jesus sayings on persecution and discipleship is that our fear of death is addressed head-on. Could discipleship be dangerous? Yes. In following

Jesus do we risk loss, alienation, death (physical or social)? Yes. Is God with us in these losses, these fears, this death? Absolutely!

The only means of addressing this elemental and primal fear is the promise that in our death there is life, in our loss there is gain, in following there is leading. What Jesus offers is not some *thing*, but some *one*: the Lord, the giver of life. What makes the risk even thinkable is the Father's spirit (Matt. 10:20), the Father's care (10:29-31), and Jesus' acknowledgment (10:32). Our feeble attempts at control—to grasp life rather than live it—can only end in loss. Following Jesus means giving up those control mechanisms and finding true life. That contemporary Christians (at least in the West) do not usually face imminent, physical danger in following Jesus does not substantively change the fact that discipleship is risky business: it calls for fundamental trust, yielding ourselves "to God as those who have been brought from death to life" (Rom. 6:13).

Sixth Sunday after Pentecost
Thirteenth Sunday in Ordinary Time
Proper 9

Lectionary	First Lesson	Psalm	Second Lesson	Gospel
Revised Common	Zech. 9:9-12	Ps. 145:8-14	Rom. 7:15-25a	Matt. 11:16-19, 25-30
Episcopal (BCP)	Zech. 9:9-12	Psalm 145 *or* 145:8-14	Rom. 7:21—8:6	Matt. 11:25-30
Roman Catholic	2 Kgs. 4:8-11, 14-16a	Ps. 89:2-3, 16-19	Rom. 6:3-4, 8-11	Matt. 10:37-42
Lutheran (LBW)	Jer. 28:5-9	Ps. 89:1-4, 15-18	Rom. 6:1b-11	Matt. 10:34-42

FIRST LESSON: 2 KINGS 4:8-11,14-16; ZECHARIAH 9:9-12

2 Kings 4:8-11, 14-16 constitutes the first of two sequential episodes in the relationship between Elisha (the "man of God," an ancient phrase referring to a wonder-working prophet [see, e.g., 1 Kgs. 13:1-32]), Gehazi (Elisha's servant), and the (unnamed) wealthy woman of Shunem (4:8-17 and 18-37). This first episode tells of the woman's hospitality towards Elisha, and Elisha's reciprocity in "providing" her a son. The importance of hospitality in the ancient Mediterranean world can hardly be underestimated. But it is not what Westerners normally think of: the entertaining of friends. Rather, it is the conversion of a stranger into a guest, as in this story.

The story is a provision miracle legend (see, e.g., Exod. 16:1-36; 1 Kgs. 17:8-16; 2 Kgs. 2:19-22; 3:9-20; 4:1-7; Mark 6:30-44; John 2:1-11), albeit an unusual one. But it also includes motifs from the traditional birth legend (see, e.g., Gen. 16:1-16; Judg. 13:2-25; 1 Sam. 1:1-20; Luke 1–2). The birth motifs include (noting those here in 2 Kings 4): a statement of barrenness (v. 14), promise of a son's birth (v. 16a), protest (v. 16b), and report of the birth (v. 17). Those motifs not included here are: the response to the protest (e.g., Gen. 18:13-14), the naming of the child (e.g., 1 Sam. 1:20) and the summary outcome (e.g., Luke 2:40, 52).

The twist on the birth legend is that the interest does not focus upon the son to be born, the one who will become a great ancestor or hero (e.g., Ishmael, Isaac, Samuel, Jesus, John the Baptist). Indeed, neither the parents nor the son is named. The interest is in the power of the man of God to broker God's patronage. Note how this story's combination of the themes of hospitality, reciprocity (giving and receiving), and promise of a son parallel Abraham's hosting Yahweh in the guise of three "men" (Gen. 18:1-15).

Zechariah 9:9-12. The book of Zechariah is comprised of two distinct parts. Chapters 1–8 are connected to the prophet Zechariah ben-Berechiah ben-Iddo (Zech. 1:1), who prophesied along with Haggai during the Persian period when the Jerusalem temple was being rebuilt after the Babylonian exile, c. 520 B.C.E. (see Ezra 5:1; 6:14). Chapters 9–14 are quite distinct from the earlier chapters in terms of style, vocabulary, and historical references. They refer, not to the Persians, but to the Greeks (9:13); the prophet Zechariah is referred to in both first and third persons in chapters 1–8, but not at all in 9–14; and the last chapters are introduced by two new superscriptions (headings): "An oracle" (Heb. *massa'*) in 9:1 and 12:1. Indeed, this is only one of the reasons some scholars conclude that chapters 9–11 are distinct from 12–14 as well.

In this passage Yahweh declares a new day for Judah. The Yahweh speech comprises 9:9-13 and is composed of the following elements:

I. Announcement of a (new) king	9:9-10
A. Call to rejoice	9a
B. Announcement proper	9b-c
C. Promise of divine support	10
II. Declaration of community release	9:11-13

The announcement by Yahweh of a (new) king for Judah speaks to the hope for restoration of the Davidic monarchy and independence from foreign hegemony. Note that it is Yahweh, and not the king, who will separate Judah from war (v. 10a-c), and it is Yahweh who will "wield you [Zion] like a warrior's sword" (v. 13). This is contrasted with the king, who is "humble and riding on an ass" (v. 9b-c). Humility is a value that means not presuming on others, not moving out of one's status, not demanding recognition. But humility is not an end in itself; rather, it is a means to gain honor by demonstrating that one fits into the group, and by not publicly grasping precedence; note the accusation against Moses and Aaron: "You have gone too far! . . . Why do you exalt yourselves above Yahweh's assembly?" (Num. 16:3). One may contrast the king in Zechariah 9, then, with David's son Adonijah: "Now Adonijah ben-Haggith aggrandized himself, saying: 'I shall become king'; and he prepared for himself chariots and horsemen, and fifty men to run in front of him" (1 Kgs. 1:5). In a strong-group culture, the impetus for leadership (or any form of prominence) should come from either the patron god or the community, not from a "power-hungry" throne claimant (see also the negative example of Abimelech in Judges 9).

The Gospel of Matthew employs v. 9 to interpret the entry of Jesus into Jerusalem on an ass (Matt. 21:1-11), perhaps joining it with the formulation in Isa. 62:11 as well. But the element that many interpreters have missed with regard to the metaphor of a king riding an ass in Zechariah and Matthew is that it may have been part of the Judean royal enthronement ritual (see 1 Kgs. 1:33, 38). Note that the Jerusalemites in Matthew 21 do not have any difficulty identifying Jesus on an ass as "son of David" (viz. a Judean monarch).

(For Jeremiah 28:5-9, see the Fifth Sunday after Pentecost.)

SECOND LESSON: ROMANS 7:21—8:6

In this passage Paul speaks to the tension of having been "delivered" (7:24-25), but struggling with issues of a physical body living in the world, with temptation welling up from within (7:21-24). For all of Paul's articulation of a new life in Christ ("set free," "in Christ," and walking and living "according to the spirit") he acknowledges here that this new life does not mean that daily existence is somehow made unproblematic. For the opposition of the new and old lives, see also Gal. 5:16-26; Eph. 2:1-10; Col. 3:1-4; one can see that the Corinthian congregation was also experiencing this tension in Paul's estimation (2 Cor. 3:7-11).

The apostle uses the word *law* (Gk. *nomos*) in numerous ways in this brief section: neutrally, positively, and negatively: "a law" (7:21; meaning a principle—evidently neutral), "God's law" (7:22, 25; 8:7; evaluated positively), "another law" (7:23; referring to the law of sin), "the law of my mind" (7:23; his higher consciousness), "the law of sin [and death]" (7:23, 25; 8:2; the hostile, coercive force in the world), "the law of the Spirit of life in Christ Jesus" (8:2; a positive life force), and "the law" (8:3; referring to the Torah). If many ancient (as well as contemporary) readers were perplexed by Paul's writings (see 2 Pet. 3:15-16), it may, in part, be due to the complexity of his arguments; but it may also be due to the variety of nuances with which he uses key terms.

What Paul identifies within himself is a powerful conflict between the "good" (*kalon*) and the "evil" (*kakos*). This he locates in the dichotomy between his "mind" (*nous*; 7:23, 25) or "inner person" (*eso anthrôpos*; 7:22), which is drawn to do good, and his "body" (*sôma*; 7:24), "flesh" (*sarx*; 7:25; 8:6), or "members" (*melê*; 7:23), which is driven to evil. The singular formulation "sin" (*hamartia*) does not refer to a specific behavior for Paul. Rather, it is an evil force that permeates his body and has him in a form of slavery (7:23). This slavery can only be broken by God's action in Christ (7:24), who sets the believers free (8:2). But one must conclude that this is not a theoretical position for him; it seems to be an overwhelming experience of what psychologists call "repetition-compulsion": a drive to replay negative experiences, despite one's conscious will.

(For Romans 6:1b-11, see the Fourth Sunday after Pentecost.)

GOSPEL: MATTHEW 11:16-19, 25-30

These two passages are connected by their focus on the theme of wisdom and the metaphors of children. In ancient Israelite/Judahite tradition, wisdom is difficult to define. It includes elements of knowledge, insight, and practical behavior (see Prov. 1:1-7). But in the biblical literature the audience is repeatedly reminded that it should be grounded and lived out in commitment to Yahweh. The following adage shows up in a variety of permutations throughout the wisdom books (see Job 28:28; Ps. 111:10; Prov. 1:7; 4:7; 15:33; Wis. 6:17; Sir. 1:14 :The fear of Yahweh is the beginning of wisdom and the knowledge of the Holy One is insight (Prov. 9:10).

But beyond the *theme* of wisdom, Jesus is identified here in Matthew 11 with the figure of "Woman Wisdom" (this precise formulation does not actually appear in any of the ancient texts; but it highlights the fact that Wisdom is a female character in Israelite/Judahite wisdom literature), depicted both in the Old Testament and Apocrypha (for example: Job 28:1-28; Prov. 8:1—9:18; Wis. 7:7—10:21; Sir. 4:11-19; 24:1-22; 51:13-30; Bar. 3:9—4:4). This connection is made by maintaining the feminine designation in Matt. 11:19, and by adapting her invitation to put on her yoke in 11:28 (see Sir. 6:23-31; 24:19; 51:23, 26-27).

Matthew 11:2-19 addresses the relationship between Jesus and John the Baptist. The rhetorical question and its answer in vv. 16-17 are a negative challenge to the honor of the crowds who gathered to hear Jesus: the failure to dance or mourn at the appropriate times are metaphors of their immaturity and shallowness. They can only be identified as mere children (Gk. *paidiois*) in the worst sense (compare 1 Cor. 3:1-4). "This generation" is virtually always a negative epithet in the Synoptic Gospels for the hostile crowds that Jesus encounters (see, e.g., Matt. 12:41-42; 23:36; Mark 8:12; Luke 11:49-50; 17:25); it refers to the Judeans in Jesus' era, since time is measured here in generations. Verses 18-19 provide the justification for Jesus' accusation. The different life-styles of John and Jesus both elicited negative responses from the crowds: John's asceticism led to accusations of demon possession, and Jesus' open table fellowship led to accusations of being shameless (a lack of attention to conventional honor and purity concerns). As radically different from each other as they were, both John and Jesus were labeled as deviants (persons out of place) by society at large. By juxtaposing the two of them as deviants, readers are directed to see Jesus as both similar and dissimilar to John.

The second section (11:25-30) is composed of three forms: (1) Prayer of thanksgiving (vv. 25-26); (2) Declarations of agency, knowledge, and revelation (v. 27); and (3) Threefold invitation and threefold rationale (vv. 28-30). While in the form of a prayer of thanksgiving, vv. 25-26 are another attack on the honor of any in the crowd who might consider themselves wise. The metaphor of revelation to "infants" (Gk. *nêpiois*)—instead of "the wise"—provides a clever twist on the metaphor of "childishness" in vv. 16-17. The evangelist also uses this word *infants* positively in 21:16 (quoting Ps. 8:2) of those who hail Jesus as king.

The declarations of agency, knowledge, and revelation (v. 27) appear unexpectedly in the Synoptic Gospels. They are more in line with formulations found throughout the Gospel of John. John also tends to intertwine the three notions:

> "The Father loves the Son and has placed all things in his hands." (3:35)
> "The Father loves the Son and shows him all that he himself is doing;
>   and he will show him greater works than these, so that you will be
>   astonished." (5:20)
> "I know him, because I am from him, and he sent me." (7:29)
> "I know my own and my own know me,
>   just as the Father knows me and I know the Father." (10:14b-15a)
> "Jesus, knowing that the Father had given all things into his hands." (13:3)
> "Righteous Father, the world does not know you,
>   but I know you, and these know you have sent me." (17:25)

These affirmations speak of Jesus as the unique broker of God's patronage. He knows, he is known, and he makes known. He does not act in the ways he does out of personal motives, but as directed by the Father.

The three imperatives in Matt. 11:28-30 are invitations to relationship: "Come to me" (v. 28a), "Take my yoke" (v. 29a), and "learn from me" (v. 29b). As stated above, these metaphors are taken from the descriptions of Woman Wisdom in the wisdom literature. She beckons to the young to enter into relationship with her because the benefits are enormous. In fact, this passage reads like a reinterpretation of the phrases and metaphors from Sir. 6:18-30:

> "Come to her . . ." (6:19)
> "Come to her with all your soul." (6:26)
> "Put your feet in her fetters, and your neck into her collar." (6:24)
> "Her yoke is a golden ornament." (6:30)
> "Search out and seek, and she will become known to you;
>   and when you get hold of her, do not let her go." (6:27)
> "For at last you will find the rest she gives." (6:28)

By taking Woman Wisdom's role, Jesus identifies himself as one who invites and includes, a classic sage, and a manifestation of divine wisdom (see John 1:1-18). The rationales are that Jesus brings "rest" (Matt. 11:28, 29) and a light burden (v. 30) in exchange for the heavy burdens of life (v. 28). For the metaphor of a "light yoke" or being "under the yoke" as a positive experience, see 1 Kgs. 12:4; Hos. 11:4; Lam. 3:27; Sir. 51:26.

(For Matthew 10:32-42, see the Fifth Sunday after Pentecost.)

Seventh Sunday after Pentecost
Fourteenth Sunday in Ordinary Time
Proper 10

Lectionary	First Lesson	Psalm	Second Lesson	Gospel
Revised Common	Isa. 55:10-13	Ps. 65: (1-8), 9-13	Rom. 8:1-11	Matt. 13:1-9, 18-23
Episcopal (BCP)	Isa. 55:1-5, 10-13	Psalm 65 *or* 65:9-13	Rom. 8:9-17	Matt. 13:1-9, 18-23
Roman Catholic	Zech. 9:9-10	Ps. 145:1-2, 8-14	Rom. 8:9, 11-13	Matt. 11:25-30
Lutheran (LBW)	Zech. 9:9-12	Ps. 145:1-2 (3-13), 14-22	Rom. 7:15-25a	Matt. 11:25-30

FIRST LESSON: ISAIAH 55:1-5, 10-13

The whole prophetic poem is 55:1-13 and belongs to the genre of "prophecy of deliverance" (see, e.g., 1 Kgs. 11:31-39; Isa. 38:4-8; Jer. 27:9-11; 32:36-44). This genre of prophecy brings the divine word of hope into the midst of sickness, destruction, or seeming hopelessness. Addressing the postexilic community of Judah (c. 515 B.C.E.), the prophet begins by repeatedly inviting (come, buy, eat, listen, delight, incline) the community to Yahweh's feast: water, wine, milk, rich food (vv. 1-3a). The banquet image as communion with the deity has a long history in the tradition (see, e.g., Exod. 18:12; 24:9-11; Isa. 25:6), as does that of a king (here, Yahweh) throwing a banquet for his supporters (see 2 Sam. 6:18-19; 1 Kgs. 1:24-25). The sharing of food creates relationship, along with reflecting the image of the gracious host's provision (see Gen. 18:1-8; Judg. 19:16-21). The object of hearing and responding to the invitation is "so that you may live" (v. 3b). What Yahweh offers at this royal banquet is not "dinner," but life itself.

The promise of deliverance resides in an "everlasting covenant," hearkening back to the Davidic covenant (v. 3b-c; see 2 Sam. 7:5-16). Judah and Jerusalem had been attacked and then destroyed by Nebuchadnezzar and the Babylonians in 598 and 587 B.C.E., taking especially the elite off to exile and ending the Davidic monarchy. After Cyrus led the Persians to overtake the Babylonians two generations later, he provided for the release of the Judahites (539 B.C.E.; see 2 Chron. 36:22-23; Ezra 1:1-4). This last part of the book of Isaiah relates to this returned community struggling to get back on it feet.

(For Zechariah 9:9-12, see the Sixth Sunday after Pentecost.)

SECOND LESSON: ROMANS 8:1-17

Throughout this passage, Paul articulates the binary opposition of two modes of life: "according to the flesh" and "according to the spirit." He indicates that, for the church, living in the mode of the spirit is the result of multiple factors; notice that he alternates between the divine and human roles in the relationship: God has set us free (vv. 2-3), we set our minds on spiritual things (vv. 5-6), God's spirit dwells in us (vv. 9-11), we "put to death the deeds of the body" (v. 12), we have received (from God) "the spirit of sonship" (v. 15), we suffer with Christ (v. 17). So life in the spirit is both choice and gift, receiving what has already been given.

The contrasts Paul brings into play here are familiar from earlier parts of Romans (as well as Galatians):

law of sin and death (v. 2)	law of the spirit of life (v. 2)
law (vv. 3-4)	God (vv. 3-4)
the flesh (vv. 4, 5, 6, 7, 8, 9, 12, 13)	the spirit (vv. 4, 5, 6, 9, 13)
spirit of slavery (v. 15)	spirit of sonship (v. 15)
death/dead (vv. 6, 10, 11, 1)	life and peace/alive/live (v. 6, 10, 13)
sin (v. 10)	righteousness (v. 10)
does not have Christ's spirit (v. 9)	spirit of God/Christ in you (vv. 9-11)

In Romans 7, Paul uses "law" in a variety of formulations (see above, the Sixth Sunday after Pentecost); and here the term *spirit* (Gk. *pneuma*) is employed with several nuances: (*a*) essence: "spirit of life in Christ Jesus" (v. 2), "spirit of slavery" (v. 15), "spirit of sonship" (v. 15); (*b*) the human spirit, life force: "our spirit" (v. 16); (*c*) spiritual, as opposed to carnal ("flesh"): "according to the spirit" (vv. 4-6, 9, 13); and (*d*) the life force of God in human experience: "God's/his/the Spirit" (vv. 9, 11, 14, 16), "Christ's Spirit" (v. 9), "the Spirit of him who raised . . ." (v. 11). The reader may quickly assume that each time Paul uses "spirit" it refers to God's Spirit, or the Holy Spirit. But this is to miss the diversity of uses, as well as to think in trinitarian terms inappropriate to the first century. Despite triadic formulas in the New Testament (e.g., Matt. 28:19; John 14:16-17; 2 Cor. 13:13; 1 Pet. 1:2), it took several centuries for theologians to formulate a doctrine of the Trinity (most notably the Cappadocian Fathers in the fourth century: Basil [330–379], Gregory of Nazianzus [329–389], and Gregory of Nyssa [330–395]).

The concluding part of this passage focuses on kinship metaphors. Being "led by God's Spirit" Paul equates with having the status of "God's sons" (v. 14) and receiving "the spirit of adoption/sonship" (*huiothesia*; v. 15; see also Rom. 9:4; Gal. 4:5; Eph. 1:5). This leads to a sequence of relationships (vv. 14-17): adoption → status as God's children → God's co-heirs with Christ. The terms "brothers" (v. 12) and "adoption as sons" (v.

15) are specifically masculine metaphors referring to the believers' new standing. This is reinforced through the metaphor of heirship accomplished through adoption: a process usually limited to males, due to the patrilineal form of descent among Judeans, Greeks, and Romans. But parallel to these metaphors, Paul also uses "God's children" (*tekna theou*; v. 16), which is inclusive. There is nothing about the status or roles in Paul's overall conceptualization that is gender-specific. In God's family, everyone calls upon "Abba, Father." (v. 15; see also Mark 14:36; Gal. 4:6).

(For Romans 7:15-25a, see the Sixth Sunday after Pentecost.)

GOSPEL: MATTHEW 13:1-9, 18-23

The Parable of the Sower (13:1-9) and its allegorical interpretation (13:18-23) are part of the larger section in Matthew on parables, the third of five major discourses in the Gospel: the message of God's reign (chaps. 5–7); discipleship (10); parables (13); in-group discipline (18); and judgment (24–25). It begins with a description of the crowds following Jesus, and that he taught in parables (13:1-3). Parallel to the other discourses, it concludes with a completion formula: "When Jesus had finished these parables . . ." (13:53; see 7:28; 11:1; 19:1; 26:1). By collecting sayings around individual topics, the evangelist has constructed five "books" parallel to the five books of Moses (Genesis to Deuteronomy).

A parable is a brief, oral, storytelling genre that provides insight into a metaphorical referent. This referent in Jesus' parables is God's reign, and the parables draw from a set of objects or experiences common to first-century Palestinian life. The tradition preserves between twenty-five and forty examples of parables in the canonical Gospels (depending upon one's definition), and a few more in the noncanonical Gospels (e.g., the Parable of the Assassin in *Gos. Thom.* 98). My working assumption is that Jesus told *true* parables, and virtually all of the changes to the parables in the direction of allegory (a decoding of the narrative elements, usually in the direction of Christology; e.g., Matthew's interpretation of the Parable of the Wicked Tenants, 21:33-46) or example story (moral lessons; e.g., Luke's interpretation of the Good Samaritan, 15:11-32) were introduced in the oral tradition, or by the evangelists, to adapt them for different audiences.

While the evangelist does not collect all of the parables he wants to tell into chapter 13 (see also 18:12-13, 23-35; 20:1-16; 21:28-32; 33-46; 22:1-14; 24:43-44, 45-51; 25:1-13), he highlights the importance of this section in a number of ways: (1) as the third of the five discourses, it is the center of the Gospel; (2) these are the first parables he tells; (3) this section is where he concentrates seven of them; and (4) he includes programmatic statements here on interpreting the parables (13:10-17, a midrash on Isa. 6:9-10; and 13:24-35, a midrash on Ps. 78:2). The organizational pattern of the seven is clearly based on clustering metaphors:

> Farming (Seeds)
> 1. The Sower (vv. 3b-8)
> 2. The Weeds among the Wheat (vv. 24-30)
> 3. The Mustard Seed (vv. 31-32)
> Baking
> 4. Yeast in the Flour (v. 33)
> Business
> 5. Buying a Field with a Hidden Treasure (v. 44)
> 6. Buying a Valuable Pearl (v. 45)
> 7. Catch of Fish (vv. 47-48)

The Sower, the Weeds among the Wheat, and the Catch of Fish all have more developed narrative plots than the other four. For each of the longer parables the evangelist provides an allegorical interpretation. The interpretations for the Sower and the Weeds among the Wheat are separated from the parables so that the narrator can have the crowd exit, and the parables can be characterized as secret information for the in-group. The interpretation of the Catch of Fish, on the other hand, immediately follows the parable since the crowd has not been reintroduced.

The Parable of the Sower also appears in Mark 4:3-8, Luke 8:5-8a, and *Gos. Thom.* 9. While Matthew and Luke make slight modifications of Mark's parable (including adapting his allegorical interpretation), *Gos. Thom.* 9 is evidently not dependent on Mark, and it does not have an allegorical interpretation. Here in Matthew's telling of the parable, the three unsuccessful sets of seeds (eaten by birds, v. 4; sun-scorched, vv. 5-6; and choked by thorns, v. 7) are paralleled by the three successes in good soil: a hundredfold, sixty, and thirty (v. 8). The most significant editorial change Matthew has made in the Markan text is reversing the order of the success numbers: Mark has thirty, sixty, a hundredfold (Mark 4:8). The effect of this is that Matthew's numbers express diversity of growth/success, as compared to Mark's sense of ever-mounting growth/success.

The allegory provides a decoding of the main story elements:

seed	=	the "word" (Gk. *logos*)
seed on path	=	one not understanding the kingdom
birds	=	the evil one
seed on rocky ground	=	one who falls away when persecuted
seed among thorns	=	one lured away by worldly cares & wealth
seed on good soil	=	one who understands and bears fruit

Instead of a parable of God's reign, the allegory speaks to a church in the second and third generations which has faced rising and falling membership, persecution, and misunderstanding. The "evil one" (demonic force) is at work in undermining God's reign. While Matthew is adapting Mark's interpretation, it fits in well with Matthew's perspective on a church facing internal dissension and external pressures: false prophets and messiahs (Matt. 7:15-20; 24:11, 23-24), "unworthy" members (22:1-14), unprepared members (25:1-13), a mixture of the evil and the righteous (13:47-50), and persecution (5:10-12, 44; 10:23; 13:21; 23:34).

Bracketing the allegory, the story works as a parable of God's reign by telling a story about common peasant farming experience: not all the seed thrown out comes to fruition. Despite all the hazards the farmer faces, a bountiful harvest comes forth. The story concludes with the images of abundant growth and harvest. Note that within the parable itself the "hazards" are not evil (as the allegory identifies them), but part of the natural order: birds, rocks, sun, thorns. The reign of God that Jesus proclaims is like the bountiful harvest which comes forth despite all the hazards.

(For Matthew 11:25-30, see the Sixth Sunday after Pentecost.)

Eighth Sunday after Pentecost
Fifteenth Sunday in Ordinary Time
Proper 11

Lectionary	First Lesson	Psalm	Second Lesson	Gospel
Revised Common	Wis. 12:13, 16-19 or Isa. 44:6-8	Ps. 86:11-17	Rom. 8:12-25	Matt. 13:24-30, 36-43
Episcopal (BCP)	Wis. 12:13, 16-19	Psalm 86 or 86:11-17	Rom. 8:18-25	Matt. 13:24-30, 36-43
Roman Catholic	Isa. 55:10-11	Ps. 65:10-14	Rom. 8:18-23	Matt. 13:1-23 or 13:1-9
Lutheran (LBW)	Isa. 55:10-11	Psalm 65	Rom. 8:18-25	Matt. 13:1-9(18-23)

FIRST LESSON: WISDOM 12:13, 16-19; ISAIAH 44:6-8

In **Wisdom 12:13, 16-19**, God's incomparability is defended along similar lines to those found in Deutero-Isaiah (see above, Isa. 44:6-8; and the Fifth Sunday after Pentecost, Isa. 2:10-17). Judah's God has no superior to answer concerning his justice (v. 13). Verses 16-18 proclaim God's character in terms of power (the exercise of control over the behavior of others, vv. 16a, 17, 18c), sovereignty (kingship, and therefore, status as the supreme patron, v. 16b), and equitable judgment (treating everyone fairly, v. 18a-b). Verse 19 articulates the effect that God has on the community in terms of kindness (v. 19b), hope (v. 19c), and repentance (v. 19d). In other words, God's character is reflected positively in the community's character.

Isaiah 44:6-8. One of the recurring themes in Deutero-Isaiah (Isaiah 40–55) is the futility of worshiping idols—metal, wood, or ceramic images of gods (see above, the Fifth Sunday after Pentecost, Isa. 2:10-17). Yahwism had a long tradition of being aniconic in worship; that is, worship without physical/artistic representations of Yahweh (see, e.g., Exod 20:4-6). The only artistic representation of Yahweh that has been excavated is on a piece of pottery from Kuntillet 'Ajrud, Israel (eighth century B.C.E.): three figures are drawn with a caption "for Yahweh and his Asherah." This evidence seems to indicate two startling things: some Israelites did employ images of Yahweh; and some worshiped Yahweh alongside a female consort. In this same vein, the Judahite writings from Elephantine, Egypt (fifth century B.C.E.), refer to Anat-Bethel and Anat-Yahu, which may indicate a female consort for Yahweh in that community (although not all scholars agree with this interpretation).

The reforms in Judah under king Josiah (621 B.C.E.) clearly indicate that the people of Judah had a variety of worship forms (local kin-group religion and state religion), including the worship of multiple gods (2 Kgs. 23:1-27), and some of those within the Jerusalem temple: "to Baal, to the sun, the moon, the constellations, and all the host of the heavens," as well as Asherah, Astarte, Chemosh, and Milcom (2 Kgs. 23:5-6, 13). So the issue of competition for Yahweh's precedence addressed in Isaiah was not a hypothetical one.

Following an extended introductory messenger formula ("Thus says Yahweh . . . ," v. 6a-b), this brief text is cast as a Yahweh speech, challenging any god to step forward and claim equal status. Yahweh begins with three parallel claims to incomparability—two declarations and a rhetorical question:

"I am the first and I am the last" (v. 6c; see Isa. 41:4; 44:6; 48:12; Rev. 1:7; 22:13);

"besides me there is no god" (v. 6d; see Exod. 20:3);

"Who is like me?" (v. 7a; see Exod. 9:14; Jer. 49:19).

These claims are paralleled at the end of the speech (v. 8d-e), as well as other places in Deutero-Isaiah (Isa. 43:11, 13; 44:7; 45:6, 21; 46:5, 9; see also 2 Sam. 22:32//Ps. 18:31). These claims come to the foreground in the postexilic community, not because they are necessarily obvious to the audience, but because Yahweh's status in relation to Judah is in question and requires defense. Yahweh's incomparability is also expressed in Hebrew names: Micah/Micaiah/Micayahu ("Who is like Yahweh?") and Michael ("Who is like God?"). And in the midst of a creation litany, we find: "This is our God! No other can be compared to him" (Bar. 3:35).

The development of monotheism (belief in the existence of only one god) was a long process in Israelite and Judahite tradition. The primary issue in most of the relevant biblical texts—which many read as monotheistic—are actually focused on monolatry (worship of only one god). The pressing question was not "Do many gods exist?" but "Does this god claim my singular allegiance?" Thus, the Decalogue does not begin with "I am Yahweh, the only god," but: "I am Yahweh, your God, who brought you out of the land of Egypt, out of the house of slavery; you shall have no other gods before [or: besides] me" (Exod. 20:2-3). In the Psalms one finds numerous declarations that Yahweh is above all other gods, such as: "For Yahweh is a great God, and a great King above all gods" (Ps. 95:3; see also Pss. 96:4; 97:9; 135:5; 1 Chron. 16:25). Israel owed allegiance to Yahweh because of what Yahweh had done on Israel's behalf; Yahweh had the status of Israel's patron god and demanded an exclusive relationship.

(For Isaiah 55:10-11, see the Seventh Sunday after Pentecost.)

ROMANS 8:18-25

In this powerful passage, Paul reflects on the present situation in contrast to what is to come, and believers' experience of the "already" and the "not yet." While he previously stated that believers are already "sons" and have "received the spirit of adoption/sonship" (7:14-15), he now says that believers long for the revealing of God's sons (8:19) and await adoption (8:23). He indicates that suffering with Christ now will be transformed into being honored along with him. This connects "taking up the cross" with benefits of God's patronage and Jesus' brokerage (see Matt. 10:16-39; 2 Cor. 1:5-7; Phil. 1:27-30; 3:10; 1 Thess. 2:14-15).

But beyond the individual believers, and even beyond the community of faith, Paul speaks of the entire creation (Gk. *ktisis*) as "waiting" (v. 19), "subjected to futility" (v. 20), "set free from bondage" (v. 21), "obtaining liberty" (v. 21b), and "groaning" (v. 22). In other words, God's created order is in the midst of the same process as the followers of Christ. Or, to put it the other way around: the community of faith is part of a cosmicwide process.

GOSPEL: MATTHEW 13:24-30, 36-43

The Parable of the Weeds among the Wheat (13:24-30; see *Gos. Thom. 57*) and its allegorical interpretation (13:36-43) are part of the larger section in Matthew on parables, the third of five major discourses in the Gospel (for an overview of Matthew 13 and parable interpretation, see the Seventh Sunday after Pentecost, Matt. 13:1-9, 18-23).

The Parable of the Weeds among the Wheat is a story of feuding neighbor farmers. It opens similarly to the parables before and after it (the Sower [vv. 3-8], and the Mustard Seed [vv. 31-32]), with sowing seed in a field (v. 24). Subsequently, an enemy comes by night and sows weeds, with expected results (vv. 25-26). In a conversation between the slaves and the householder, the slaves are confused by this development; but the owner identifies the source of the problem as an "enemy," and he decides to wait until harvest time before separating the weeds from the wheat (vv. 27-30).

The plot line in *Gos. Thom. 57* is very close to Matthew's narrative. The differences in details are all relatively minor: (1) Matthew's characters are a "householder" and "slaves," while Thomas's are a man and an unidentified group (they could conceivably be family members, neighbors, day laborers, or slaves). (2) In Matthew the householder discerns the work of an enemy, but in Thomas the enemy remains hidden, and the man only discerns that a weed problem has developed. (3) In Matthew the slaves and the householder each have two speeches in the dialog; in Thomas the conversation is compressed into one speech by the farmer. And (4) Thomas does not include the final note about bringing the wheat into his barn. But the most important distinction between Matthew and Thomas is not in these details: Thomas does not include any allegorical decoding of the parable parallel to Matt. 13:36-43. This indicates that the parable did circulate in the oral tradition without this allegorical interpretation (this is also true of the Parable of the Sower in *Gos. Thom.* 9).

As Matthew tells this story, it is an allegory for which the reader is provided a precise decoding in vv. 36-43, afforded only to the inner circle of disciples:

sower of good seed	=	Son of Man (v. 37)
field	=	world (v. 38a)
good seed	=	children of the Kingdom (v. 38b)
bad seed	=	children of the evil one (v. 38c)
enemy sower	=	devil (v. 39a)
harvest	=	close of the age (v. 39b)
reapers	=	angels (v. 39c)
gathering weeds	=	rooting out sin and evildoers (vv. 40-41)
burning weeds	=	the "furnace of fire" (v. 42)
the barn	=	the Kingdom of their Father (v. 43a)

The clear concern of the evangelist is the purity of his group/s. The group is polluted with members who are not truly faithful, or have false agendas (see, e.g., Matt. 7:15-23; 13:47-50; 22:1-14; 24:11, 23-24; 25:1-13), and the devil/evil one is to blame for the contamination of the group. In the first century, Mediterranean people were very concerned with the "who question" when it came to causation. The whole world was perceived as personal; when either success or disaster occurred, the central question was, Who caused this to happen? whether that might be another human, a demon, an angel, or God (see, e.g., Matt. 5:45; John 9:1-3). So the "enemy" in the story, whether allegorical or not, is to be expected as an explanation for this agricultural disaster, rather than an impersonal wind blowing seeds into the field, for example. The evangelist advises a strategy of waiting for God's emissaries to rectify the situation later, rather than encouraging the church trying to take care of it sooner.

In his magisterial work on the parables, Bernard Brandon Scott has argued that this story does not originate with Jesus, but was always the church's allegory about in-group purity, even without the precise allegorical decoding of Matthew (*Hear Then the Parable* [Minneapolis: Fortress, 1989], 68-70). Since most scholars do not believe the authors of Matthew and Thomas borrowed from each other, this would mean that the allegory developed in the oral tradition between the time of Jesus and the writing of the Gospels. This is certainly plausible, since one may interpret the focus as boundary-maintenance. And, as Scott points out, Jesus was concerned more with *boundary crossing* than boundary maintenance. He concludes that there is no clear referent to Jesus' proclamation of God's reign.

I think this interpretation, however, is too focused upon the sifting out and burning of the weeds (v. 30), interpreted as judgment in v. 42 (and also in 3:12 and 13:49-50). What if the metaphorical focus is not on purity or judgment, but on God's reign being like the discernment and clever-ty or judgment, but on God's reign being like the discernment and clever-ness of the farmer who cannot be undermined by his enemy? In agonistic cultures such as those in the ancient Mediterranean, feuding between fam-ilies is a commonplace. But the farmer's advantage is that he is too crafty to be deterred by hazards put in his way. Like the seed that produces despite the hazards of birds, rocks, sun, and thorns in the Parable of the Sower, the farmer can succeed despite his enemy's plot. Unlike the slaves, he can see past the weeds to the wheat, and knows how to get what he wants. The farmer's discernment and astuteness has parallels, then, to the discerning treasure finder (Matt. 13:44), pearl merchant (13:45-46), and fisher (13:47-48).

(For Matthew 13:1-23, see the Seventh Sunday after Pentecost.)